by Jana Dennis

PALMYRA STREET

Neighborhood Story Project
Red Rattle Books/Soft Skull Press
New Orleans, Louisiana
Brooklyn New York
2005

D1361721

Other books from the Neighborhood Story Project

Before and After North Dorgenois by Ebony Bolding
Between Piety and Desire by Arlet and Sam Wylie
The Combination by Ashley Nelson
What Would the World be Without Women? by Waukesha Jackson

Series Editor: Rachel Breunlin
Graphic Designer: Gareth Breunlin

Palmyra Street
ISBN 1-933368-30-6
ISBN-13 978-1933-36830-6

© 2005 by the Neighborhood Story Project

Let us hear from you. www.neighborhoodstoryproject.org.
Neighborhood Story Project
P.O. Box 19742
New Orleans, LA 70179

Soft Skull Press, Inc.
55 Washington St, Suite 804
Brooklyn NY 11201
www.softskull.com

Distributed by Publishers Group West
www.pgw.com

Text pages produced on 70 lb. Lynx Opaque, Smooth Finish,
donated by Weyerhaeuser Company, Fort Mill, South Carolina
Tango Coated Cover, donated by MeadWestvaco, Stamford,
Connecticut, manufactured in Covington, Virginia
Printing and binding donated by WORZALLA, Stevens Point,
Wisconsin USA

DEDICATION

I dedicate my book to my block of Palmyra Street. I want them to see that our block is not just negative. They have some positive things and people. I really want them to know that we are not just neighbors, we are a grateful community that doesn't take each other's kindness for weakness. When we receive, we give and when we give, we receive. Our family on Palmyra cares about one another and is willing to help at any time. We believe if you give a blessing, you will surely get a blessing.

ACKNOWLEDGEMENTS

First I want to thank God for sparing my life another day. He has allowed me to go through a lot of issues and I thank Him for that because I have learned and am still learning a lot about His messages.

I want to thank my mother for sticking by my side through thick and thin times while my book was being written. I also want to thank her for reading and looking over all of my stories. She had some wonderful ideas and great advice.

I want to thank our class: Kesha, Ebony, Ashley, Sam, Arlet, and Ceirod for the laughter and enjoyment we had in class. Thanks as well to Ceirod for taking photographs of Chief Rob.

I want to thank Rachel and Abram for pushing us that extra mile to work hard at whatever we do. They have taught us to be diligent. Thank-you to Rachel for editing my interviews and to both her and Abram for helping me take photographs.

I want to thank my neighbors Zelda and Melvin; Pooky and Spug; Chavonne and Nora; Tamaya, Korielle, and Keniqua; Mark Damico; Jose; Paul Tuzzo; Crazy Paul; and Mr. Ricky. I'd also like to thank Chief Rob for doing an interview.

I want to thank my family, including my grandmother Eva; my brothers Eddie and Joseph; and my sister, Joya.

I'd like to also to thank Steve Gleason, Lauren, Lashana, James, Chavinne, church members, visitors, relatives, friends, and finally myself for all the time, effort, photos, advice, good luck, interviews, money, and support throughout the year. I really appreciate all you have done for me. I know you are so excited that we accomplished the goal of publishing my book.

TABLE OF CONTENTS

PART I: MY FAMILY

My mother Ms. Price, my two brothers Joseph and Eddie, my little sister Joya and me. What are we? We are a family. Not just a family, but a group of people who believe in sticking together. We are backbones for one another. We go to church every Sunday. We try to do everything positive. My mother always kept us in different activities so that we would keep out of trouble—not that we were bad or anything. There are just so many dangerous and strange things happening in this world. That's how we became Indians of the Golden Arrows.

My mother works at a Head Start pre-school and one day the Chief Rob of the Golden Arrows came to visit the pre-school children. They did a little show for them with dancing and singing. When they were finished, they had a little luncheon in the classroom. They sat down and talked about how they became Indians. It was a tradition for them because their fathers and grandfathers were Indians before them.

My mother was interested in becoming an Indian. She came home and called a family meeting. Usually when she calls a family meeting it's about safety, sex, health, or activities. She's very open when it comes to family discussion time . We sat down to talk about becoming Indians. We agreed to mask Indian. We started sewing and beading day after day for almost a year. I would call my mother the "miracle mom" because she sewed five suits in a year.

We were able to mask for almost four years. We still have thoughts in the back of our minds wondering if we are going to mask again. Maybe some day, but right now we are doing different things. Joya's into ballet and tap dancing. Joseph is a freshman weight trainer for the girls' basketball team, as well as a track, football, and golf player. He's also a fashion designer. Eddie plays football. My mom is a full time parent, and a wonderful teacher and cook. And I am a full-time writer, cashier, and singer.

Do you see how busy our family is? It seems like we never have time for each other. That's why my mom sets that 9 pm time for us to be inside. It's our time to enjoy one another's company. But even if we didn't have a curfew, we would still make time for each other because we are a family and that's what families do: stick together.

INTERVIEW WITH JOYCE PRICE

My mother is Ms. Price. She likes to be called her middle name, which is Joyce. She grew up in Midcity and graduated from Warren Easton. She worked at a gas station, Eckerd's, and Popeye's before she went back to school when I was young. She works as a teacher at Oak Leaf Head Start.

My mother worked hard raising four children by herself, trying to be the mother and the father at one time. My soul never was hungry, my feet were never bare, my clothes never needed washing, and my family never was homeless. My mom takes her family out a lot. We like to try new restaurants like King Buffet and New Orleans Seafood. She wants us to try things. She brings us to church every Sunday and encourages us to get involved in different activities. This woman raised and showed me how to be independent. She showed me how to work for what I want.

She's a giving person; even in the neighborhood she feeds everyone. She really doesn't mind cooking a meal to feed a soul. There's this thing that's happening to my mother. It's just little children keep coming to her when parents need help. But sometimes she gets close with the child, starts taking care of that child, and then the situation changes and she doesn't see them anymore. She said whatever child comes to her, she will take care of it until something comes up. "My blessings is going to come one day."

While I was doing this interview with my mama, my brothers and sister kept interrupting because they wanted to be a part of the conversation. We ended up talking about what our family is going to be like in the next few years. My mom wants us to leave home and go to college. She always says, "Don't be like me, be better than me." I know she wants the best for us. Sometimes I don't think she realizes what a high standard she's set.

Jana: Where were you born?

Mom: New Orleans, Louisiana. Charity Hospital.

J: Where did you grow up?

M: I grew up in New Orleans on Orleans and Lopez.

J: What was it like growing up in the neighborhood?

M: Everybody was family-oriented. My grandmother lived on one side of the double and my mom lived on the other side. Across the street my uncle stayed. Around the corner, my aunt stayed. They were my daddy's brother and sister.

My mom had seven sisters. And my uncle, he cooked every Sunday. Every Sunday everybody know, if you want to eat, go there. For the holidays everybody go there. Everybody just go to his house and it's still that way. He owns three houses on St. Peters and still stays in the house where my grandmother lived.

J: Did you have good experiences there?

M: Yeah, we had good experiences. I grew up with four teenage uncles and they told us that Easton park was our park, and we used to tell children to get out of our park, because we believed that was our park.

J: How did y'all believe that was y'all's park?

M: They told us, we didn't know no better. We were like eight, nine, and they said, "That's your park, go tell em to get off your swing."

J: You liked doin that?

M: I didn't know no better then. I know better now.

They used to pluck us and pinch us—they don't do that to y'all now.

J: What did your parents do for a livin?

M: You mean as far as workin?

J: Mmhm.

M: My father was a construction worker and my mother used to work at a cleaning factory. Now she does housework. He never was one to come to around on weekends or nothing like that. He's still the same, he stay to himself. He just never really was family-oriented.

MOTHERHOOD

J: What was it like to become a mother?

M: Oh, it was exciting. I didn't know I was having twins until I was on the delivery table, but it was exciting.

J: Will you tell the story of our birth?

M: Jana and Joseph's birth? Okay, I was seven months pregnant and I was sitting in the clinic waiting on my appointment and my pants were wet. I went to the bathroom [and when] I came back, my pants were wet again. I went to the front, and I told the lady, "Somethin wrong," I say, "because every time I sit down, my pants are wet. I'm wettin myself." She said, "Baby, your water broke." They rushed me upstairs and put me on a monitor. My nurse came and checked me, did my vital signs and said, "You're fine." The next day they came to check the baby—how you got a baby heart up here, and a baby back down here? And I said, "I don't have the slightest idea."

She said, "You must be havin two babies."

I said, "They told me I was havin one big baby." It came out I had two. I stayed in the hospital seven days before I had them and they stayed in the hospital twenty-two days after they were born. Jana was healthy, she was just small and she had jaundice. Joseph had breathing difficulties and he has asthma now from it, but other than that they had all their fingers and toes and eyes.

J: How was it raising twins?

M: It was easier than raising one.

J: How?

M: My twins never did cry, they never cried for my attention. When I had Eddie, Eddie was a crybaby.

J: Why? Because we had each other?

M: I guess. I guess that's what I got from it. When I had Eddie, Eddie cried for everything. I couldn't leave the room.

Rachel: Can you talk a little about the connection that Jana and Joseph have? Pain and just knowing how each other is feeling....

M: Well, when she has a bad headache or something, the first thing Joe will come home and ask, "Jana your head was hurtin today?" She say, "Yeah. " And he has the same thing. Like when her cycle come down, he gets her headaches and he gets the sleepiness from it. He got hurt on the football team and she come home limping. Nothin wrong with her leg, but she was limpin and she didn't know why. But he had got hit playing at practice and sprained his leg.

J: How do you balance raising children and having time for yourself?

M: I really don't have much time for myself. Last year, I made a New Year's resolution to take out time for myself. I take out time and I go to plays. I take out time and I just go buy myself something. I stopped buying for them all the time, and I started buying for myself sometime. I had to make myself because everything was just, "My kids, my kids, my kids."

But, ever since they were little, nine o'clock is really their bedtime. After nine o'clock is my time. And that's been since they were born. A lady in Charity told me, "Baby, if you put them on a schedule, they'll be on a schedule." And if they're in the house and nobody in here but us at nine o'clock, everybody in here asleep.

It gets hard sometime when I'm the only parent and they mad with me because they don't have nobody else to talk to. I have to hear the blame—I have to hear it all. You want to say, "Okay, baby, I'm sorry." But then you have to stand strong sometimes and say, "I got to let em grow up" and "Okay, I have feelings, too, and can't just do just anything."

I try to [have good communication] because me and

my mom never did. We are very open. We be in the car and we talk about everything. I mean, I've never hidden anything from them. I'd rather them to know than not to know.

PALMYRA STREET

J: Why did you decide to move in Midcity?

M: In the Midcity area? Well, when I moved from in Gentilly, Midcity was closer to my job and it was closer to everybody's school, so that's why I moved in this area.

J: Why did you move to Palmyra Street?

M: I found a house!

J: How do you take care of other people in the neighborhood?

M: Oh, man. Where do you want me to start? Let me see. Combing hair, changing clothes, dancing, cookin, I mean—um, I can't give a lot, because I don't have a lot, but what I have, I'm willing to share. So, I think that's why God kept me where I'm at. Because I don't have no problem with giving. I don't have a problem with sharing whatever I have.

J: When did you learn to cook?

M: Oooh. I learned a lot from my grandmother and I learned a lot from, I don't know—

J: Experimenting.

M: Yeah, experimenting.

J: My first time cooking, I cooked a pot of grits and I burned them.

M: But that's all right, you kept trying. I didn't stop you. I want everybody to learn how to cook. You've got learn to feed yourself.

J: What's you favorite recipe?

M: My favorite recipe. What? Gumbo?

J: Yaka Mein.

M: Yaka Mein. I cook them whatever they want to eat. I cook a lot of stuff I don't eat.

J: She don't have no recipes, she just do it. I'm telling you. She says, "Now, get the meat, get the vegetables, get the sauce." She just start throwin stuff—she don't have no recipes!

CONFRONTING VIOLENCE

J: Do you worry about the violence in the neighborhood?

M: Yeah, I worry about it but I mean, it's going to happen. I've been to the point where I had to get out on the street to keep my son out of a gang, because they were trying to initiate him in it. They used to follow him and jump on him, and he used to go all out of his way.

I called the police two or three times and they told me unless they can catch them in the act, there was nothing they could do. He never bothered nobody and they never thought he had back up. I had to get on the phone and called some people. I had people from that block to that block. You hate to have to do things like that. But all those guys that were trying to initiate him in those gangs, they are either dead or incarcerated. All of them.

CHURCH

J: What were some of your memories of church when you were young?

M: When I was young, we went to church every Sunday. My mama brought us up in church. I sung in the choir and when I grew older, my brother, he got away from it, but I always stayed in church.

J: How did we choose the church that we belong to?

M: My church, it's a family-oriented church. My mom came from Franklinton Louisiana, most everybody in that church is either from Franklinton, Bogulusa, or Mississippi—right in that little circle— so everybody in that church knew each other from when they were little. So it's really still family oriented. It's waning out but we have a few left.

J: What do you want us to get out of church?

M: I want you to know there is a greater power and throughout your trials and tribulations that you will not always be alone—whether you have a human person, but if not, there's always a spiritual being, so you can have someone to talk to strengthen you. A greater power.

Rachel: Do you find a sense of community within the church?

M: Yeah, some. I mean, we're getting a lot of people since we've gotten this new pastor. He's young and we have a lot of new people that are coming to the church that aren't really family-oriented. We try to keep it there, but it's waning out to a new generation.

J: What's the role of music and singing in our family?

M: We sing it all. We sing gospel together. We sing blues together. We sing the hip hop. We do it all. We get in here, we move the table out the way and we dance. They think I can't move no more because I don't dance in front of them. I'm not that old. I can still move when I want to move. We have fun together. I want them to be family oriented and I want them to be open with their children, so I have to be open with them, you know. Maybe they'll be a little more open with their children than I am with mine, you know. I want them to be giving.

MARDI GRAS INDIANS

J: What were your memories of being an Indian when you were young?

M: Oh, when I was younger, I thought it was—

J: Dangerous?

M: No, I thought it was a certain type of people that did it. I didn't think anybody could participate in it. You know, when you don't know the background of it, like riding on the floats on the Zulu.

J: How did you decide to get into the Golden Arrows?

M: For you guys to experience something that you never experienced before. I wanted you guys to take advantage of doing things that was positive and try new things. I never wanted you to say, "Well I wish I could have done it and I didn't do it."

My co-worker Donna introduced me to Norman. He was doing Indians. I went with her because her daughter wanted to originally do it, but she didn't want to sew. She thought somebody was going to sew for her, and they told her, "You have to sew for yourself if you want to participate, you have to sew." So I sewed; she didn't sew. My kids participated but hers didn't.

R: How long did it take you if you had to do five suits?

M: The first year I did four suits. And it was a year. It was a year. My auntie sewed up the basic stuff and I did all the rest of it. And then the next year, it was another year. They enjoyed it and I enjoyed seeing their smiles on their faces. It was positive and, you know, it was with the community. They was proud. They had their little suits on and it made them feel good.

J: What did you learn from the experience?

M: I learned the different Indian cultures and how it came to New Orleans and why they mask Indian. It's really spiritual, it's uplifting, and it's really passing on from generation to generation.

R: How would you describe the Golden Arrows?

M: Oh, man, they wild. They good people, but they wild. They're people from all different areas—West Bank, projects, uptown, downtown, from everywhere, so you have a lot of different—

J: Personalities.

M: A lot of different personalities. A lot of different attitudes. You have some people that go to church, some that don't go to church. You have some that drink, some that don't drink. I mean, it's a whole lot of people together doing one thing, but different. Everybody got along when they was doing the Indian thing, everybody was one And just after that, every-

body went their own way. But when we was together, when we went to different bars to meet different Indian groups, we was all as one.

Nobody knew we was Indians were around here, because we took our suits out of the house, in the car, and we was uptown.

J: We got dressed on St. Peter and Lopez.

M: You let people know that you're Indians, you have different Indians that have different attitudes.

J: They be hatin on you.

M: So, I didn't want them to ever have to watch their back, just because they participated in something.

BALANCE

J: How do you balance everything?

M: I pray and I take vitamins every day, but sometimes I just be whipped. Like today—I had a rough day today, but Joya has to go to dance class for six and then I have rehearsal for seven.

J: Thank-god she got Jana to cook.

M: I'm not going to get back home til 10:30. But everybody's able to cook for themselves, even if Jana don't cook.

J: Everybody be dependent on Jana.

M: I came a long way. My mom was never really home. My mom was always at work and I was always responsible for my little brother. I had to cook, wash clothes. I decided I wanted to be home with my children. I wanted to be at the PTA's. I wanted to be there whenever they did something. I wanted to be there whenever they needed me to volunteer. I wanted to be there. I wanted to participate in their life in school. My mom never had the opportunity to do it. It helps them. And it encourages them to do better in school and to be better people. I've got teenagers and I don't have no problem with them wantin to hang out all night. I have no problem with them using drugs or fightin people just to be fighting. I think I'm blessed. And if they did, they know what the consequences is so I don't have no problem with that either.

R: What are the consequences, Jana?

[laughter]

J: A long talk. A whuppin. Punishment. No phone. I think punishment hurts more than a whuppin. A punishment by the simple fact of not goin nowhere. In your room all day—ohhh! That would kill me. Eddie, he's just lazy. Mama tell him he's punished: "All right."

M: I have to take the game from him. I have to take the X Box from him. And then when he gets back there and he gets too comfortable and he's punished, I make him go outside and that makes him mad even worse, cuz he don't want to be outside.

[laughter]

M: Take the sweets away.

J: Take the Debbie cakes!

Eddie: No, no! [laughing]

GROWING UP

J: How has your relationship with your children changed over time?

M: They think they're as grown as me. They want to do what they want to do and they want to do it, and it's not going to work. Jana is under the impression that she can never be told no. [to Jana] Stop beatin on me! Joseph wants to be grown. He wants to do what he wants to do, when he wants to do it. He's a young man, so I have to be on his level and talk to him about females and respecting them and respecting himself as far as becoming a father early. He doesn't want that; he wants to go to college and play ball. You can't go to college with a baby. I have a can in my room, it's full of condoms, all colors, all flavors, I don't discriminate. If they're gonna do it, I tell em to use em.

J: Where do you see your children in five to ten years?

M: I should be in my house with my husband and no children.
Joseph: Who's your husband?

J: I'm not going to go nowhere, I'm sorry.

M: You're going to be in college. Five years from

now you'll just be graduating from college. Them two will just be going to college, so I'll have the house to myself. Joya might be the only one home.

J: I'm not goin nowhere.

M: You're going to school.

J: I'm going to Xavier.

M: Stay on campus!

J: No! You have to pay to stay on campus.

M: Okay, get a job.

J: Where you see yourself in five to ten years, Joe?

Joseph: I'm going to college and then I'm going to play ball.

J: What you going to college for?

Joseph: Art school.

M: You thought he didn't know, huh? Uh huh. Hatin on you.

J: You like art?

Joseph: Mmhm.

E: I'm going to school for natural resources.

[laughter]

M: What happened to becoming a judge?

E: That's a long time in school.

JANA AND JOSEPH

On January 19, 1988 I was born. A beautiful blessed child who deserves to be in this world. That's not all, not just me, but my twin Joseph, too. My mother had two little creatures. We weren't just little, we were tiny. I mean, I was two pounds and my brother was three and half pounds. We was so small we could fit in a shoe box. My grandma use to hold us in each one of her hands. My grandma was so shocked to see how small we came out. I was hospitalized for three weeks and my brother was hospitalized for four weeks. I was in their for jaundice and my brother was in there because his body wasn't fully developed. We were little for a long time.

My mother told me when we were just four months she use to shape our heads. You know, when you are at least two months premature you are born with long heads. Well, my mother said she didn't want our heads looking like acorns so she molded our heads with her hands in a circular motion so they looked normal like everybody else's. But those days are all over. On January 19, 2005 Joseph and I celebrated our seventeenth birthday with ice cream and cake. That night he had a basketball game around the corner by Sacred Heart gym.and I went on a date. My friend Quincy took me to Five Happiness Restaurant to eat and enjoy some Chinese food.

WHO AM I?

A beautiful black woman
A young female who likes to learn
from other women
A smart person
A diligent person
An honest person
A sweet person
A quiet person
A neat person
A not too much mean person
A drug-free person
A happy person
A writing person
A singing person
An outspoken person
A friendly person
A kind person
A loving person
A caring person
A helpful person
A mindful person

John McDonogh Prom 2005

A JOYFUL CHURCH SERVICE

Sitting in church on those cold benches listening to the preacher. The church audience is nodding their heads or shouting amen. The little children are sleeping while their mothers or fathers are holding them. The parents are mad because the little children are drooling and their laps are wet. The ushers are patiently waiting for the normal to happen when someone shouts and catches the Holy Ghost. Some they can calm down by fanning and giving them some water. The preacher teaches about, "How to receive your blessing." The church audience is very touched by the sermon. Some get so excited that they starte jumping, shouting and crying. After the service, the church is humble. Everyone just walks quick and quietly out the door. Well, maybe a few conversations, but that's it. It's like everyone can't wait to go home and repeat the message the preacher preached to someone else.

MASKING WITH THE GOLDEN ARROWS MARDI GRAS INDIAN TRIBE

I became a Mardi Gras Indian in the year of 2001 when I was thirteen years old. My sister Joya and I were little queens, my twin Joseph was the spyboy, my younger brother Eddie was the second spy, and last but not least was my mother, who was the first little queen.

Those positions that I named all have a responsibility when your tribe is out in the street: The first spy boy stops traffic so the Indians can pass. The second spy boy has the first spy boy's back so nothing will happen to him. The big queen protects the little queen. If a little queen can't handle being challenged in dancing, then big queen has to hurry jump in and take her place.

Masking seems easy, but its not. Being an Indian you have to have patience. In order to mask you have to have a perfect costume. You can't come out there half-stepping. Having part of your costume ready and half not is going to make you look silly and stupid. It takes a long time to sew an Indian costume—about a year. It takes at least a month to sew just a patch. A patch is a piece of canvas sewn with a lot of beads, sometimes sequins too. You have to take your time and string every last bead onto that piece of canvas. It takes hours to sew a broach. A broach is a smaller version of a patch. All it has is sequins and a few beads.

We mask on Mardi Gras. We start from La Salle, and go across the street to Shakespeare Park to take pictures with friends, family, tours, and fans. It makes me feel special; I enjoy all the attention on me.

Having someone to come up to you and say, "You are so beautiful and your costume looks nice," means so much to me.

GOLDEN ARROWS CONTINUED

Indians challenge each other in dancing and the outcome of the Indian suits. When I meet another Indian, I forget about everything around me and just start dancing. I'm not acting like me. I'm acting like an Indian.

After the Golden Arrows mask Uptown, we pack up and get into the trucks and head down to the Claiborne bridge where we mask for a little bit until we decide to mask down Orleans. We listen to all kinds of music and smell all kinds of barbeques. While we are trying to focus on what we are doing, it's hard not to get side-tracked because there are so many people and things to do.

Once we make it to St. John Bayou we are done for Mardi Gras Day. It's usually about five o'clock. We mingle around with each other, undress and just chill. My mom has pickles, olives, okras, and Gatorade waiting on us to make sure we don't cramp up. She always has a bottle of aspirin waiting on us, too. We are not tired but our feet are. After we take off our costumes we sometimes challenge in dancing against one another.

We mask other times during the year, too. We enjoy ourselves when we do shows. In May, we normally do the Jazz and Heritage Festival. We walk around the Fair Grounds and maybe spend an hour with the little children. Around St. Joseph Day we go around doing pre-schools. The little pre-K children are so excited and you know some of them might be scared. We sing fun songs they enjoy like "Indian Red" or "Shadow Water Your Mama."

After a few years, I grew out of masking. I just didn't want to do it anymore. I got tired of walking and being around all of those crazy people who follow in the second line. I guess when I have a child she or he will take over my masking Indian spirit.

AN INTERVIEW WITH ROB JOHNSON

Robert Johnson is the second chief of the Golden Arrows. I met him when I started masking at thirteen years old. I masked with him for almost four years. I was living in Gentilly then and we used to meet at the Bayou. He would line us up by positions. He taught us to be hard up and handle our business. He always believed that school came first and didn't mind helping you with homework. Once he got on you about your academics, then he would go to your sport skills and check out how you are doing by popping up to attend your games. He was a role model when I was young. He could never get me to mask again because I'm not up for all that sewing, but maybe one day my children will keep the tradition alive.

We had a party at our house and invited Chief Rob over to talk to my class about being a real Indian. He's a great storyteller and a wonderful singer. We asked him lots of questions and he told us stories about life as a Mardi Gras Indian.

BEGINNINGS

People ask me, "Why do you mask Indian?" There is a history of why we do this. Back in slavery time, when they had the Underground Railroad and a lot of the slaves ran away—they ran on the Indian [territory]. Well, the owners know they couldn't go [there] because there was going to be trouble. The blacks that migrated with the Indians, they learned their culture. We mask Indian to show the homage and thanks to the Indians for letting our people stay with them and migrate on their land.

It's spiritual. Before we do anything, we do the Indian prayer. And at the end, we sing the prayer. Have you ever heard it? If you listen to it, it will tell you the meaning of it. [It's] the spirit [of] the Indians that have died and passed on. We pray to you and you're not forgotten. If you ever come to an Indian practice, you'll feel it.

Practice starts up the third weekend in September after the Young Men second line. It's challenging one another from a different gang. If you come, you'll say, "I got to go see this again because it was amazing." The way they tried to out-dance each other. And the signals they throw. "I don't understand nothing about it, but I feel it." That's how so many people get adapted to it. They're like, "Oh man, I don't know what that was, but, you know, it's deep."

The tradition has been in my family a long time. My grandfather was the [Big Chief of] Black Eagle. It was hectic. The closer it got to Mardi Gras, it was like no one goes outside and plays. Everybody had a job. If you couldn't sew, [but] you was old enough to thread a needle, [you'd] hang em up in the curtains with the thread hangin down. The whole back of the sofa would be laced with needles with the thread hangin, so as you're sewing the beads, you can grab one already threaded. You have a big card table with

the top cut out with your canvas material over and everybody sit a while, sewin a section. My grandmother thought we was crazy just spending money like that, but she enjoyed it. She looked forward to us comin out every year. She loved the colors.

When my grandfather passed it down, he gave it to me after he called a hoomba. A hoomba is a submit; it's when you bow to your chief. Now, it's a pretty thing if you ever see it on Mardi Gras. All the feathers go towards the ground and your chief and your Wildman stand up. All the feathers bow towards him. You only do that when no other gang is around. The Big Chief taps the person who he is making the new chief. I stayed with Black Eagle, but as years went along, I went in Golden Arrow.

My grandmother still stay in the neighborhood [where] I come out. Back in the day it used to be a troubled neighborhood. You had to be a rough little cookie to come up in that neighborhood. The neighborhood is quiet now. The only loud noise you hear is if a guy with a stereo passin. The Indians out there on Mardi Gras Day, you know, the whole neighborhood just light up. They look for Mardi Gras. They look for the Indians from the door—for someone to come challenge me. The second liners are normally family members, friends, people who've helped put my costume together, [and] guys out of the neigh-

borhood. They will follow you. "Hey, he come out of the neighborhood, I'm gonna follow him."

[Once you've masked], you're recognized throughout the year. Because that's who you are; that's who the neighborhood see you as. Your position is you. Like Derek, he's spy wherever he go. "What's up, Spy?" "Hey Chief." "How you doin Queen?" I'm an account manager for Weiser Security Service. I work on computers nine to five. At six o'clock I'm in front of the TV sewing with the news on. It's relaxing. If I have a problem or have a bad day, I can just go sit at the table and just sew and my mind is eased. Listen to a little music, have a little high ball or something—next thing you know, whatever had me upset is not even on my mind.

BROTHER TIMBALL

When [my grandfather] came up maskin in his younger days, it was about being tough. You couldn't be no chump and mask no Indian, because you would get whupped or they would run you home. Every tribe that met back then fought—it wasn't no pretty sight. I was there when my parents had to pick me up and run towards the neutral ground sidewalk to get me out of the way, because they're fighting. You know, literally fightin. Back then, the suits wasn't as big as they are now. You know, they were nice little petite suits with feathers and designs, but now

they're enormous suits.

When we was comin up, my grandfather used to meet an Indian with the Golden Arrow [called] Brother Timball. We stayed around the corner from one another. We came up on Sixth and Dryades and he was on Daneell and Sixth. He was a big man, and he was a schoolteacher. He was the nicest guy you ever wanted to meet—until the week of Mardi Gras. The week of Mardi Gras: Oh, he'd be humbuggin. Play the music loud. He's drinkin. Hootin and hollerin. Cuz he's getting ready. So, the neighborhood call the police. "Mr. Timball over there makin that noise again. You know, he goin to be trouble. You know what he do every year. Y'all better come get him!"

The police knew him well. They knew once he put that suit on and start drinking, Brother Timball changed. And guess what? He used to carry a hatchet. And when they sing the song, "A Hatchet in the Head," Brother Timball would split your head. If you don't get out of his way, he will hit you with the hatchet. They then gave Brother Timball warnings. One day, the police even walked with Brother Timball. He left so many Indians with their heads busted on the street, a day or two before Mardi Gras the police used to lock him up in jail. He got so bad that two or three days before Mardi Gras, he wouldn't come home. He'd be somewhere else and he'd leave from there.

But Brother Timball was not the meanest in his gang. Herbert was. Herbert was his Wildman. And when I say Wildman, Herbert was supposed to be in Mandeville years ago. Mind gone. I mean, you could be a spectator—he'd just come run over you. He had two antlers that were just so pointed and he used to just stick you [with them]. I mean, he cleared out the whole block. With Herb up front and Brother Timball in the back, that was a gang you didn't want to meet. And you couldn't run from him. Because guess what? He'd come find you. "Oh, you see me comin and you want to turn another way!!"

BUILDING YOUR SUIT

I want to mask every year. Wish that Mardi Gras was more than once a year. It's just that we don't get to put the suits on that much. You know, it took all that time and money to make it. You raise the money out your pocket. You take a little at a time. Now, it's some Indians that have been masking for a while, they get a grant. Some kind of way, they make a proposal and they get a grant and they do it every year. I've never gotten a grant yet. The average working guy—every payday he'll go buy twenty dollars worth of beads this week. Next week he'll go buy fifteen dollars worth of thread, needles. He get his canvas and he draw the pictures that he wants to bead, then he starts sewing. Within a year you spend about a hundred and fifty dollars on beads.

The highest thing masking is feathers. We wear plumes. Downtown wears turkey feathers and we wear the big ostrich plumes. I wear anywhere between twelve to fifteen pounds of feathers. A pound costs a one hundred and eighty some dollars a pound, so I'm lookin at almost two grand or a little better with taxes. The place in New York that we get our feathers from, you send a money order every week, every month until you pay off your feathers and then they ship you the kinds you want. We have that arrangement up there with that because we've been dealing with them so long.

Now, believe it or not, plumes are like a flower—they will bloom. If you keep a feather on a suit on the wall, the feather will wilt. You sprinkle baby powder on it and put it in front of a fan and turn it on, come back, and them plumes will bloom.

It's just different things that come to you, that you'll be sitting and like and think, "I'm going to do that." I might look at an old cowboy book or a Western movie, or any movie and you'll see something and you'll go, "You know what? I'm going to try to remember this and sketch this." Then you just make a whole story about it, you know.

A little kid [named Jessie] draws for me. [He]

used to go to school with my son. One day, I looked in his folder and he had nothing but cartoon characters that he drew. I say, "That's good. How you traced this?" He said, "I didn't trace it, I drew it." I gave him a picture and said, "Let me see you draw that." He drew it just like the picture [and] I made an offer.

MARDI GRAS

Normally [at the last Indian practice], everybody wear something on their head. You're supposed to wear the color that you will wear. But they never wear that color. You put a feather in your head of another color. You put a feather of the color of the spyboy. Your spyboy might have your colors. "Oooh, yeah. So you're going to wear green." And the medicine man wearin green, you know.

You can't sleep the night before. You're hyped My own mother has to be like, "Look, turn back, you haven't left home yet." When I put on the pants and jacket and shoes, you just feel so hyped. And you got your crown standing outside on the mannequin and you just feel it. Once your crown is on your head and the whole block start jumpin up and down and the drums start rolling—that's it. Whatever else

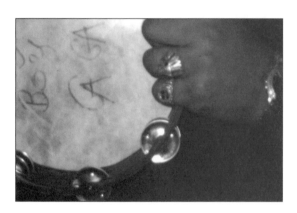

was around you—gone. I think I be possessed. The feathers do something to you. Your mind on: I want to see the next Chief; you know, "Let's go get em."

I'm Golden Arrow and around the corner there's another guy with the Wild Magnolias. He cannot walk on the block where I stay in his suit. And I can't walk in his block unless he's out and I can go meet him. But just walkin past when I'm not out yet is disrespectin. Normally, we have the corners shut down with the Indians. You know, the spy at one end and the Wild Man at the other.

It's a religious feelin when we sing on the street. When you meet somebody, and you're lookin him in the eyes, you're in that trance. It's the ringin of the tambourines and the beat of the drums—everything just flow. You know, "Damn. I didn't know I was spittin the words like that!"

DEALING WITH OUTSIDE INTERESTS

[One year there was a white guy who] made a suit, but didn't have a tribe. He came out by himself. He had a whole bunch of colors—red, green, and yellow. You remember? Guys thought, "He's disgracing the culture." They literally just went over there and whipped him. Next year, the guy made another suit. He got punished again. But after that, nobody bothered him. It was a white guy. Ever since then, he's been maskin. Nobody bother him. They meet him. You know, I guess they said, "He paid his dues." We look forward to seeing him every year.

But he's not the first white Indian we ever had. The first one was Flynn. He's from London. He's affiliated with my grandfather. He met my grandfather because my grandfather was a seaman. Worked on the riverfront and used to go, you know, all over. Flynn used to see my grandfather sewin on the ship and he was always fascinated. "How you make a whole picture—you know, look like a painting with beads—just sewing one by one?"

The first time, he put on a suit, same thing happened to him. And he still came every year and he got whipped—paid his dues. He became a Chief. And right now, you go to any practice and you ask anybody who was the first white chief, they will tell you Flynn. Still to this day, everybody make it their business to go shake Flynn's hand.

He sponsors Black Eagle. To this day, he buys the chief all his plumes and his material. Every Mardi Gras he comes down. He don't mask anymore.

But he love the Indians. He takes pictures of em and everybody goes to him. I don't care how many years—even the guys that hit back then, go up to him and shake his hand because they're friends. Back then they thought it was a mockery.

[It's hard because] a lot of times we have been exploited. I go to the Jazz Fest every year. They're sellin posters [of my suit and] I don't get a dime. That's why, when Indians see real photographers, they'll fold up. They won't let them see their whole suit. Now, if they do it, the council will go after the people. They could buy the poster, see who published it, and they go sue em. We copyright our suits. Now, if we see this design again displayed anywhere without your notice—"Hey, get your lawyer."

IT'S LIKE CERTAIN SONGS...

You want to do "Shadow Water?" "Shadow Water" [was a song] that me and this other guy Emmanuel—God bless the day, he's dead now—used to sing. He come from Tootie Montana. He was young, wild, and he made a beautiful suit, you know

what I'm sayin? But he didn't know how to listen to authority. He left Yellow Pochahantas and after awhile, Jake from the White Eagles named him and gave him a gang. And guess what the name of his gang was? Trouble Nation. They made a song about him: "Nothin But Trouble."

Mardi Gras Day, [his gang] comin from downtown. They're young. They be jumpin all up and down. Me, after eight or nine blocks walkin with that suit on I'm like, "Lord have mercy, give me a drink. Let's take a break. Let's stop at this bar! Sit

down for a minute." But when you see that gang comin, you best get up, because they're not gonna give you no break, they're gonna bring it to you. Emmanuel had a mouth piece. He know how to rib ya. He knew how to talk about you. He used to call me Big Chief Barry White—I hated it. You know, and he'd sing it in a song to you. He'd look at you, and he'd start singing about you. You're like, "Man, sing about somebody else. Anybody else." But, Emmanuel was a character. I miss him.

If you ever come to Indian practice, all the chiefs be back there in a hole. My spyboy in the center of the floor—he gonna meet [another chief's] spyboy. And they will dance and challenge. The chief who's holding the practice, he's singing in the back. He got all the drums and tambourines. Now the chief comin through door, he's singin. He's got his tambourines and things—let everybody meet. The chief comes in the back with the other chiefs, and they sing. Now, you know, we'll sing the same song and he'll be singing and then [someone] will tap him on the shoulder—that means let him cut in and he'll sing.

Emmanuel could take any song and put your name in it and just roll with it. See, anybody can make a suit, but you've got to know how to play the game. Emmanuel knew how to play the part.

CHIEF ROB ON MARDI GRAS DAY

PART II: WELCOME TO THE 3300 BLOCK OF PALMYRA

In July, the year of 2002, my family and I moved on the 3300 block of Palmyra Street. We moved from our old house one block away because that house flooded, destroying all our furniture and personal things of sentimental value that could not be replaced, every time it rained. It was also infested with rats and roaches. I mean big, bold rats; the kind that know you're watching and stare right back at you. And the roaches—oh my God—they were the really big ones that flew in aggressive formations, attacking like acrobatic war pilots gone kamikaze. Ha Ha Ha. Imagining "killer cockroaches" sounds like the strip from a horror movie "Set in the sticks," huh? That's exactly why my family and I had to move.

The day we moved it was my mom, my twin brother Joe who is exceptionally big for someone his age, my younger brother Eddie who really doesn't enjoy participating in any activities that are physical-ly exhausting unless it's football or basketball, and my younger sister Joya, the baby in the family. Try to imagine us moving an entire household of belong-ings— literally carrying them up the street from house to house. Although it was a lot work, we had fun, too. Besides, we were happy to finally move up out of the jungle.

The houses are so old in Midcity on Palmyra Street. They are French-made houses like back in slavery times. They are very similar to one another. The house that I live in is leaning to the right and it's going to fall straight down in about five years or so. The painters who painted the houses back then did a wonderful job. The only difference is in color. There is a tree, plant, or a small bush planted by each house. My neighbor Ms. Nora says it's too hot to have all that, "Got dawn sun in our face." She repeats, "I'm too black for that shit."

Although our neighbors are crazy we still get along with each other. Now that we have lived at 3313 Palmyra for two and a half years, I think we have learned everyone's names and where they're from. That's very important to know the kind of people you're around. We have a mixture of races in our neighborhood: African-Americans, Latinos, and Vietnamese. We all try to speak to each other. We also respect one another.

There are a lot families on Palmyra so there are a lot of children. There's always someone outside their front door watching out for someone's child. Safety is very important on Palmyra Street because there's a school on the corner and small children are always crossing the street. There is a 25 mph sign up but the fast crazy drivers don't care.

With so many children in the neighborhood, there's plenty of cooking going on. Children on Palmyra Street always have a hand out and mothers are always willing to give a plate. I know my mother cooks on every holiday, including Saturdays and Sundays. The neighborhood enjoys her cooking. The big meals are only on Sundays. She cooks pork chops, greens, cornbread, and yams. We're in the kitchen eating until we hurt ourselves, unless we have money and eat out.

Once you move on Palmyra you are very welcome into any of our homes. We will always take care of each other no matter what. That's why we consider ourselves "The Palmyra Street family."

MS. NORA'S CHILDREN

Ms. Nora is my next-door neighbor. She was living in the house when we moved in. She's a very nice lady who believes in having fun. Lately, she doesn't have much free time because she's going to work and school. If you ask what she's wants to drink when she has some time off she'll say a Bud Light beer. That's her punch, milk, and water. Ms. Nora has two sons: Corey and another one that passed away. Corey is twenty-three years old. He has four kids with Chavonne: Korielle, JJ, Lil Corey, and Tamaya.

Ms. Nora's household includes Mr. Jim, her future husband, and two little girls she is helping to raise–Tamaya and another neighbor's daughter named Keniqua. They are some nice little girls. Ms. Nora should feel blessed. Mr. Jim always asks her if she wants or needs something. To me, he makes her feel so special. Ms. Nora probably does feel special. I know I would.

Tamaya attends Fisk Howard Elementary and is in the first grade. She loves to read the kind of books that pop up when you open them, but she doesn't like to write. If the teacher gives her homework and she doesn't want to do it, she will lie to Ms. Nora and say, "I don't have no homework." I know she's not telling the truth because my sister Joya goes to the same school and she has homework everyday.

Tamaya, aka Maya

I always ask if she has homework and she always tells me, "No." Then I'll tell her to bring me her book sack. I'll tell her, "Open it and take out your folder and open that too." She usually has homework in every subject. I went over her homework with her and she gave me the answers. I rewrote it nice and neat; so she could rewrite it herself and get a good grade on it.

Tamaya loves to play outside with her friends Korielle, Keniqua, and my sister Joya. If you ever happen to observe Tamaya long enough one day you will catch her posing or dancing. She loves to shake her little apple bottom. If any type of song comes on she would probably get on the ground or get on the wall and start shaking. I had to ask her, "What are you doing? Stop shaking, you need to learn your ABCs."

She says, "I already know them."

"I don't care— just stop popping your booty. You are too young to be doing something like that."

She says, "I sorry, Jana. I promise I won't do it no more." She'll go inside and get something more positive to play with. Now when she pops she makes sure I'm not there to see her.

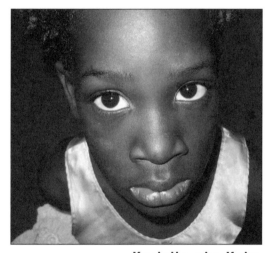

Korielle, aka Koko

Keniqua, aka Moan

Keniqua Willis is one of the neighborhood's favorite children. She tries to speak to everyone who passes on Palmyra. She has her own way of talking to people She goes all out of her way screaming your name saying, "Hey, hey, hey! What you doing?" If you are sitting on the porch and your head is down or you are writing, she will ask about a thousand times, "What's wrong? What's the matter? Do you need a hug?" Even though adults in the neighborhood are older, they still need a hug every now and then, and Keniqua is right there to give it to you.

CHAVONNE: CHANNELS 4, 6 & 8

In Mid-City, Palmyra is the street known for violence. Palmyra is just a dangerous street. Drugs, jealousy, and abuse happen inside and sometimes spill outside onto the block. I don't like it, but there's nothing I can do about it. I stay inside a lot when I'm home alone and I'm also gone a lot with work and school. I hear about the events that go on mostly from the news or neighbors.

Every time something happens guess who's there? Ms. Nora's daughter-in-law Chavonne. She receives all information and details about the crime story. Is it murder, abuse, drugs, or even a fight? She has been doing her job since I have lived on the block. Everytime she comes to visit her daughter Maya, she already knows what's been going on. She says, "Long as something's happening, I'll be there."

AN INTERVIEW WITH MS. ZELDA

Ms. Zelda stays across the street from me at 3314 1/2 in the blue and white house. She is thirty-two years old and has twelve children. Her oldest, Cleo, is sixteen years old and her youngest, Lil Melvin, is one year old. Cleo attends John McDonogh with me. She's good at braiding and twisting hair. Ms. Zelda loves to cook for her kids—not no little meals either. She cooks at least two meals in one. She'll serve macaroni and peas or steak and gravy with rice and string beans.

In her free time she drinks a beer or two and plays cards or dominoes. I should say, "used to" because she doesn't anymore. Now she attends church every Sunday for seven o'clock. She recently got baptized in the Pontchartrain Lake. I didn't know that much about her life when I did this interview, but I learned that she plans to change her whole life.

RAISING CHILDREN

I grew up in New Orleans, Louisiana with my mother. I know [my daddy] but I don't deal with him. I'm the first child. I watched the other kids so my mama could go to work at a hotel. As days went on, I was missing more and more [school]. I remember one time when my mama lights got shut off and I didn't have no hot water. I boiled water to wash the clothes in the sink. But my childr—I was about to say my children—they went to school clean. In eleventh grade, I dropped out to help my mama raise the rest of my brothers and sisters.

Sometimes I get mad because my mama always tells me about how my sisters and brothers finished school and I didn't. [I want to say,] "You're not giving me credit that I dropped to help you with these children," but I can't talk about it. Me and my mama get along fine, but if I want to talk to her about what I've been through, or what I'm feelin—mm mm. She ain't tryin to hear that.

I sacrificed a lot, because guess what? I could have been somebody. See, I really look up to Jana. I should be showing Jana how to look up to me, because I'm older, you understand? But I look up to Jana because she's trying to be an author. She can do it. It's a mind over matter thing.

I could have been somebody, but I got these children I got to worry about now. I had my first child when I was twenty years old. My mama tried to take her from me, but when we went before the judge, the judge couldn't find no where that I was an unfit parent because I gave them my last and I still give them my last. I have twelve children. I buried one [who was stillborn] and I got the rest of them. Every last one of em has a different personality and sometimes it's hard and sometimes it's easy.

When I moved out of my mama's house, I stayed in the Iberville Projects for thirteen and a half years. I got put out, [because I went to jail and couldn't pay the rent]. I was homeless [and] I had to give my children up. The state took them, but they're not with the state, they're with their daddy. I'm just starting to get them back. The man that I'm living with [now] was in penitentiary for five years and somebody told him the situation that I was going through. He got this apartment and put me and the five kids that are back with me in it. Cleo, Cory, Cleveland, Craig, and Melvin. It's still not enough room for me to get the rest of my children back.

PALMYRA STREET

This the first time Jana ever listened to what I'm going through. She never knew how it was, you understand. But I feel like if I had problems, I could go to [my neighbors]. We used to go to Nora's house and sit down for little while. She just took to [my daughter] Keniqua for some reason. That's my baby. We call her Moan. Nora saw what I was going through and that I was trying and she came and asked me if [she could adopt Keniqua]. I took her as a Good Samaritan and said, "Yeah." I knew that somebody was doin better than me.

If I was a boy—to be honest with you—I probably wouldn't be here sitting talking to you right now. Because I know what type of boy I would be. I'd probably be out here with the boys—you know, doing me. It's called protecting my family. Surviving. "You're not going to touch my turf. You're not going to touch my family." I ain't worried about no turf, because I don't have a turf, but I have a family. Turf— that don't mean nothing. But my family mean a lot.

Above: Ms. Zelda and Ms. Nora

Right now, I'm trying to get me a job and trying to move. I had [a job] that was payin me nine dollars an hour at the Convention Center. They laid me off because they say they didn't have no more work til Carnival, but then when I called them around Carnival they didn't need nobody. It's hard, but I'm a strong black woman. I know I could make it. I just want to try to get my babies back. That's it. Once I get them back, I know one thing my life is going to complete. Even as old as I am, if you are around your children, [they'll] make you feel young. I always feel young, me.

THE CORNER

The most popular spot for the boys to hang out is the corner of Palmyra and Rendon. Why? I don't know. It's probably because they have nothing else to do or it could be drug dealing. That could just be a place where they do social gathering. It could be possible that the corner means so much to those boys they just can't leave it. I know what it is: they are boys trying to be down. They try things they normally don't do, like smoking and drinking. They don't care about being on people's property.

As I walk by one guy says things like, "What's up Shorty?" I ignore him like I always do. One time, his brother jumps in with his silly self and says, "Why you always trying to play me? I know you want me." I keep walking.

He looks to the corner while pulling up his pants. "Man, forget her." The police pull up and I guess they didn't like how he was acting. I was wondering what was going on, but I was too scared that he would blow on me. Although we are cool, and kid around from time to time, John still has his moments.

The police don't scare them. They are hard. They stand like stones.

MS. G

It was early in the morning—about two o'clock. My mother started screaming my name. "Jana! Jana! Wake up, Ms. G. just shot her boyfriend!"

I was just waking up. My mind wasn't functioning right; what my mom had said didn't flow through my head. So she said it again. I kind of came back to my senses.

"Jana, find Gennie, Gina, and Mami some shoes and clothes." Not sure what was going on, I jumped out of the bed and grabbed all my clothes out of the closet to see what they could wear. I picked out sweat pants, shirts, and slippers and carried them outside. It was dark. The streetlights were on. I could barely see Ms. G's daughters standing around the porch. They were yelling at Ms. G while she sat in a police car, "Why did you do that?"

I had known Gennie for a couple of years. We used to walk to school together in the morning. I invited her to my sixteenth birthday party and spent the night at her house afterwards. We talked to her mom as we were getting ready for bed. I don't know where she was from, but she spoke English with a Spanish accent. In the weeks that followed my birthday, I would see Ms. G's boyfrend Ricki coming over to visit, and remembered how she said it wasn't hard to raise her kids by herself.

I looked at Gennie now and didn't know what to say. I gave my mom the clothes and asked her what was going on. And she told me she was sleeping when she heard some one holla, "Neil!" Neil lived in the house next to ours. My mom went outside and Ms. G was across the street saying, "I shot him. Yes, I shot him, and what are you going to do about it?" Ms. G said, 'Neil, you can call the police. I'm not going nowhere. I am going to take my charge like a woman."

Ricki was on Neil's porch, bleeding all over the place. He was shot in the jugular vein in his neck and on the left side of his heart. His whole face was covered with blood. He was covered with so much blood he started choking. The paramedics couldn't do anything for him. Ricki died on the scene. When the police arrived her children started crying because they knew what was going to happen next. The policemen searched the house but didn't find any weapon. They asked Ms. G, "Where is the gun you shot him with?"

She responded defiantly, "I don't know, bitch, you find it."

By the time I got outside, the ambulance had already taken Ricki away. Tears were running down Ms. G's face while she was looking towards her children sitting on my porch. Gina said, "Mom I love you but you was wrong for that. I'll never forgive you for what you did." Gennie said, "Mom I love you. Why you did that? Look at you, you are on your way to jail and that's not a good place for you. That's not where you belong. Mom, please please please don't leave me. I really need you. You mean everything to me."

Mami didn't say much of nothing. She was just there crying.

Ricki's funeral arrangements were set up in Covington, Louisiana. Ms. G got to see him for the last time. She was supposed to be sentenced to ten years for first-degree murder, but she only served a few months with probation. We heard that Ricki had hit her and she pulled the gun in self-defense.

That early morning was the last time I saw Gennie. She dropped out of school and went to stay with her grandmother while her mom was in jail. Ms. G and her children ended up moving because Ricki was the landlord's cousin. Mr. Antonio didn't agree with the situation and when he found out [Ms. G wasn't going to prison] he was so angry. He told her, "You have two weeks to move out or your stuff will be put on the street." They moved within due time and never came back to visit or anything. I guess they are satisfied with their new home and neighborhood. Ms. G's final words were,"People make mistakes in life, but now it's time to move on."

ICE CREAM TRUCK

When the ice cream truck passes the little girls Maya, Koko, and Keniqua are standing at the curb waiting for someone to purchase them some ice cream. They scream "Hey! Hey! Hey! Stop! Stop! Stop! I want some ice cream!" But the truck keeps going and Maya says, 'Forget them" while Keniqua keeps dancing. She's dancing so hard her little braids were flopping in the air. Her little booty was going left to right dancing to the tune. They gave up trying to make that stupid ice cream truck stop. They finished playing but hoped the ice cream truck will pass again.

DOMINOES AND CARDS

Melvin, Spug, and Zelda love playing this game. This game brings excitement to the table. All you hear is "Cover your hand," "Bow face," "Bow face," "Don't let no one see your hand." Melvin always claims someone is cheating just so he can win. Then after he wins, he doesn't want to play any more because he feels that he has proven a point, whatever that is. It's not only dominoes that they will play, but cards too. In the evening, when I come home from school, they might be out playing pitty pat, tonk, or spades. Spug is always trying to win. He finds everyone's mistake in the game and let's them know. We can hear them playing late into the night.

BILLY THE PIZZA MAN

This man is a popular man on Palmyra Street. He speaks to everyone —especially my mom. He hollas "Ms. Joyce!" about a hundred times a day. In Nicaruaga, he worked for Somoza, but after the Sandanistas overthrew the dictator, he sought asylum in the United States. He said he feared for his life. "I don't like the communistas." In New Orleans, he works at Domino's Pizza and brings the neighbors pizza. If he brings pizza on Sunday the neighbors already know it's for Eddie because he's Billy's favorite buddy. Billy's grandson Bryant is always calling Eddie so that they can all feed the pigeons together.

NEIGHBORHOOD BOYS

MIKE

The boy who sits on the blue porch across the street is different. He shares everything he has. He's willing to help people when needed. He doesn't mind giving little children a dollar every now and then. He's very handsome. He graduated from Fortier Senior High. He loves playing dominoes with Ms. Zelda's boyfriend Melvin. He dresses nice with nothing but Rock-a-Wear. He loves the girls and women. He's now looking for a beautiful girl with a nice body. Not only that, but someone to talk to, too. A friend that he can trust and can spend time with.

STEVE

The Impresser. He tries to holla at all the girls he sees in the neighborhood. Of course, they turn him down because they think they're too cute for him, but they just don't know—Steve has a great personality. He believes in pleasing a girl not sexually but naturally. Just giving her every and any thing she wants.

KEVIN

Kevin, on the other hand, is very quiet. He's the more relaxed one. He just lets girls come to him. Kevin plays dominoes with Melvin, too. Kevin walks and thinks a lot. He hardly has anything to say. He

sometimes goes to Fisk Howard's school yard to play basketball. All he does all day is chill with Melvin, Steve, and Mike. Those boys always hang together.

LAVONNE

Lavonne has a baby girl named Aaliya Davis. She's so pretty. Her eyes are gray. Her skin complexion is like caramel. Her hair is so long and silky. She will be one in the month of February. Lavonne makes sure his baby is well taken care of by buying her clothes, diapers, and wipes. He gets along very well with his baby's mama Arianne. They have their ups and downs, fuss and fights but always take time to solve their problems. Lavonne enjoys being with his new family and plans on having a basketball career.

AN INTERVIEW WITH PAUL TUZZO

Mr. Paul stays on Palmyra Street two doors down from our house. He's originally from Brooklyn, New York, but has been working in the restaurant business in New Orleans for a long time. He owns his house and wants my mother to buy our house and then sell it in three to five years. He's fun to hang out with and a little flirtatious.

IMMIGRANT EXPERIENCES IN BROOKLYN

Jana: Where did you grow up?

Paul: In a neighborhood in Brooklyn, NY called Flatbush.

J: What did your parents do for a living

What did my parents do? I like to say they were in the iron and steel business—my mother ironed and my father stole, but that's not the truth. My mother was a homemaker. In order to tell you what my dad did, I'll have to tell you the beginning of us. My dad came to this country in 1913. He was thirteen years old. He came with his brother to New York—Ellis Island in New York where all the immigrants went when they came into New York City. I think every port probably had a debarkation point, but Ellis Island is probably the most famous in the United States, if not the world.

His mother had died in Italy and his father was already over here. The [rest of the] family couldn't afford to take care of my father and his brother, [so] they came to the United States earlier than anticipated. In New York, my dad's father sent him to school long enough to learn to speak English, which was always broken. He couldn't read and couldn't write, but he had to be one of the smartest persons I've ever known.

He started off working for his father in Little Italy with a fruit and vegetable wagon—two horses and a wagon full of fruit and vegetables. He lost the horses, the wagon, and the fruit to the dice with two other teenagers. They became infamous gangsters—Lucky Luciano and Bugsy Siegel. I don't know if you've ever heard of em, but they were pretty wild. He had to go home to his father and tell his father, "This is what I did." They went down to Mott Street and my grandfather spoke to the guys and made arrangements to pay them back the money which only amounted to about eight dollars. I asked him how much and he said, "I had to pay seventy-five cents a week." I said, "How much were you makin?"

"Fifty."

Later my father got involved in construction and worked on some major projects in the United States: the Empire State Building, the George Washington Bridge, the Lincoln Tunnel, the Hoover Dam. For most of his life he worked on what was called steam shovels. They were operated on wood and coal. He could put anything you wanted anywhere you wanted.

Rachel: How long did you live in Brooklyn?

P: I lived in Brooklyn practically my whole life. I grew up there. We moved out of the neighborhood we were in when I was like thirteen, fourteen years old. My dad worked away from home a lot. He was home maybe once a week or once every two weeks. My mother was left with the responsibility of taking care of us and he was concerned of the elements that were moving into the neighborhood. He was afraid that there might be some problems, so they moved us to upstate New York.

J: What are some of your favorite memories of childhood?

P: Going to the World Series games in '53, '54,'55,and '56 with my dad. Playing baseball in front of the house.

J: What's your favorite team?

P: My favorite team is the Yankees. Playing baseball in a car park in front of our house with my father. And I remember the ball being hit towards the car and I jumped and caught it before it went through the windshield and came down on the hood of the car. I didn't get hurt but the driver jumped out of the car—and this was like mmm, 1952, does that give you a sense of how old I am? In 1952, I fell onto the ground and it startled him and he woke up and he got out of the car. He didn't put his jacket on and there was a gun hanging under his shoulder.

MOVING TO NEW ORLEANS

P: How did I get here? My car. I've been a waiter or maitre d' for years—sometimes I think I was a waiter at the Last Supper. I was thirteen years old when I started working in a hotel. I don't know how familiar you are with an area called the Catskill Mountains. Within a fifty-mile radius there were five hundred resorts. People come there for vacations— predominantly Jewish people from New York and Jersey, from Pennsylvania and Boston. They're like cruise ships on land. You can check into a hotel and everything is included: three meals a day, your lodging, shows and entertainment. I'm talking about some of the biggest names in show business that you've ever heard—on stage–every single night. I had the opportunity to meet a great many entertainers. That's what I did there.

I came down to visit a friend because I wanted to move from New York. I wanted to get out of the cold and I wanted to get out of what I was going—directly or indirectly. So I came down here to visit some friends. I spent two weeks here. I went home and thought about it. Sold what I could, packed what I could, and got in my car, turned the rear view mirror around and headed south. September will be thirteen years.

R: What appealed to you about New Orleans?

P: What appealed to me? Not necessarily in any order. The history, the architecture, the food. The people. The beautiful women.

J: What kind of food?

P: Actually anything.

J: Seafood?

P: Yeah, I see food, I eat it. Yeah, I love seafood. I love all the ethnic food that surrounds us. I love to cook. I picked up pointers on making stuff that I had never heard of until I moved down here, incorporating what I did know into what I'm learning. Making it a combination.

J: How did you become a cook?

P: I'm not a cook; I'm a waiter.

J: Yeah, but you say you enjoy cooking.

P: Yeah, I enjoy cooking.

J: How did you learn how to cook?

P: I thank my mother for that. And in some parts my father. My mom was responsible for taking care of my brother and me on her own. The responsibilities had to be shared. We had chores. One of the chores was making dinner—being in the kitchen with our mother and helping her and watching what she was doing. And when my father came home on weekends, we knew he'd be cooking. My mother was a great, great, cook—my father was three times better. Three times better.

BUYING A HOUSE ON PALMYRA

P: I had been searching for a house. I hadn't liked what I'd seen and my friend Jeff and I were riding around and came by here and saw the house. I checked it out and kind of liked it. I asked the neighbors about the neighborhood and they seemed pretty impressed with it.

J: How long have you been living here on Palmyra?

P: Five years.

J: Can you describe this neighborhood?

P: It can be very loud at night sometimes. Yeah. Have you ever had a car pull up in front of your house with that rap music on and your walls start to vibrate because the bass is up so loudly. I consider it noise. I don't consider it music. I remember I was here about two months. Some guy pulled in front of our house and left his door open and all his windows were down. The music was just blaring and my walls were just vibrating and I came out and said to Neil, "Is it against the law to shoot a radio?" And the guy caught on and turned the radio down.

J: How many people live in your house?

P: Just me and my dog.

J: How many you have?

P: One.

J: You like your dog?

P: Yeah, I like my dog! The rest of the neighborhood's not too thrilled with it but I don't care. Between us, now, I think she's full of shit actually. She'll run up and down the fence when people are walkin by, and she'll leap and they'll swear she's gonna go over. But, on the other hand, if I want to let her out on the back deck at night, you got to turn the light on. Which leaves me to question, "So if I leave the lights off at night and I'm not home [and somebody] breaks in, they're gonna square away with everything?"

J: How do you feel livin on Palmyra?

P: I like it.

J: Do you feel safe in your home?

P: I got two guns and a Rottweiler. Do you think I'm safe?

J: Are you scared?

P: I'm not scared. I'm just protected.

J: Do you consider this neighborhood dangerous?

P: It can be. But we're responsible for it. So, in order to turn it around we have make sure that it's not going to be dangerous anymore. Didn't your mom just put those numbers in front of your house? On the curb? Or was that Nora?

J: That's Nora.

P: Okay. That's a step. It's a small step, but it's a step. We're responsible for making the neighborhood safe. We don't have to tolerate what comes into the neighborhood if it's going to be a threat to the safety of the children who play in the street or any one else.

COMMUNITY INVESTMENT

P: I see the potential for this block turning itself around and becoming not exactly a garden spot, but more than it is already. It has the opportunity and it has the potential. We have to work together. Maybe arrange getting together, having a meeting about what we think needs to be done on the block. When I first moved here, I told Neil, who lived next door to me, "We have to clean the block up in order to appear serious to City Hall." If we make a complaint that we need something done here and they drive by and see the streets and sidewalks dirty with litter all over they are not going to take us serious. They're going to think to themselves that we don't care.

I want to use something as an example because of the environment that we live in. You know, it's a predominantly an African-American block. Look at some of the movies that we see dealing with blacks. They're [portrayed as] the criminal elements [and] the camera scans [to show] litter filling the streets. It gives everyone the impression that maybe that's how we live; that's how a black neighborhood lives. It's now how we are as individuals. We have to stand up and do something about it. We have to clean up the streets. Get a sign that says, "Don't litter." We c an get that from City Hall—you saw how I had to fight to get these signs out here—the stop sign and the school zone sign. We have to continue doing it. We have to fight for ourselves. We all pay taxes one way or another, so we're entitled to do that.

Don't separate us because we're not a Garden District neighborhood or an Uptown neighborhood that has more expensive homes than we do. Our homes are important to us, too. The people who live on this street are just as important as they are on St. Charles Avenue or Napoleon or Magazine or anywhere that we go. Everybody puts their pants on the same way. Everybody pays their fair share of dues the same way. The majority of us on this block work. I know [Ms. Price gets] up every day and goes to work. We're responsible. We're responsible for our families, we're responsible for ourselves, we're responsible for our obligations, but in order to be heard, we have to have one voice, one fist. Not in a violent way, of course.

J: Okay. What are your important experiences on this block?

P: My important experiences with this block? Getting my ass on the floor that night that woman shot her husband. One night about three o'clock in the morning, my girlfriend's niece woke us to tell us that she heard gun shots. So I grabbed my robe and my gun. I put the gun in my pocket and I came to the door. I could see there was something going on outside and dialed 911. They said they already knew about it and they were on their way. I stepped outside. I guess the woman across the street got pissed off at her old man. He was running and she put two in him and killed him.

He died between my fence and the house that was owned by the other guy. He said, "We got to sell this house." It was like three-thirty in the morning. I don't think anybody wants to buy it right now, do you? Give it a day or two.

I was pissed. I was really, really pissed. You know, if you're going to shoot somebody wait until like noon so you don't have to wake me up! It's like three-thirty in the morning and she's shootin. Of course, I had to check my truck to be sure that—she was a good shot, she hit him twice. Boom! Boom! And she got him.

R: What are some of the things that you really like about Palymra?

P: Well, like I said, the people. I like the architecture. When you walk outside later, look at the houses and you'll see how similar they are each other. This house and my house are like sister houses. And I like that. I like the architecture. I'm researching the history of my house. Find out who had it.

R: When are you thinking about selling it?

P: In about three years. I"ll be about ready to retire by then. And that's it.

R: Where are you going to go?

P: I don't have any idea. I'm not going to go to Chicago; it's too cold.

R: It *is* too cold. No tropical islands?

P: Oh, yeah, if I had a beautiful woman under my arm. Why would I go to an island alone?

HAIRCUTS ON THE PORCH

Inside my house, all I heard was a little roaring noise. It would stop and then pick up again. It was such a loud and disturbing noise, I decided to go outside and see what was going on. The porch was crowded with children and I knew it was haircut time.

Our stepfather Nikki was the one cutting hair. When an occasion or holiday comes up, my brother Joseph always goes first. While he's cutting his hair, Nikki talks to Joseph about his life and real life situations. I mean, he used to be real hard on my brother. I really appreciated that because it made him a better person.

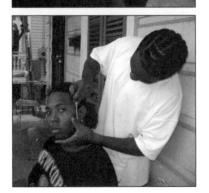

THANKSGIVING BREAK

Palmyra felt very empty. It was breezy outside and the trees were shaking. A few kids were sitting on the porch wondering when my mom was going to finish cooking. My Palmyra family was inside trying to finish up the stuffing, seasoned turkey, mouth watering yams, delicious sweet potato and crispy apple pies, cheesy macaroni, and buttered cornbread.

After Thanksgiving dinner, the big and little boys went under the Fisk Howard school yard shelter to play basketball. They played all afternoon. When they finished, I was nice enough to bring each one a bottle of water. They went inside to get cleaned up and when they came back outside, the music was playing like it was some type of DJ. The little girls Korielle, Maya, Butter, Wholly, and Keriquia were dancing. I mean their booties were shaking left to right. Their little heads were jerking with their bodies. The neighborhood started drinking and partying to the music. The block was no longer quiet.

Like usual, we went to get our Christmas tree the next day, It's a traditional thing. Every year we try to rotate colors. This year our tree was blue and silver. We snowed the tree with frost then placed the silver ornaments and put some blue Christmas stuff on there, too. We wrapped our presents with blue and silver wrapping paper and went outside to plug up the lights. When I heard Mr. Ricki say that, "The got dawn Saints better win or else I'm going to pick another football team." Everyone around started laughing, even Ms. Nora.

CAR FEELINGS

I was alone on the porch when I noticed the cars and trucks looked like they had expressions on their faces. The white Ford truck that belongs to Paul looks confused and doesn't know what to do. My mother's white Galant is drunk from all the driving last night. He's probably still tired. Mr. Darren's gray and black van looks like he's just stuck and can't move at all like he has some type of bone disease. The blue car that belongs to Mr. Lamar is still mad because he's not insured. They gray car that belongs to Mr. Billy the Pizza Man is just so happy because he's running for the last ten minutes. He's now ready to pull off to go deliver some pizzas. The blue Grand Cherokee Jeep that belongs to Nora is shocked because no one has driven it yet. He's so used to different people driving him, he's very surprised about how much sleep he's gotten recently. He doesn't know what to do.

WHITE CHRISTMAS

My family gathered on St. Peter and Lopez streets in a red and white house filled with Christmas joy. At the end of a long day, the little children were excited again because they saw a little ice outside—something like sleet. They ran outside not even wearing coats and started making little ice balls, trying to throw it at each other. The ice was getting thicker but soft. It was the first time in fifteen years it has snowed in New Orleans. The crystal white snow fell out of the blue sky. The children started making bigger and harder snowballs. My whole family ended up in the snow. They came back inside to get warm and continued playing cards and eating. They even drank until they got drunk and couldn't take no more.

The next morning the sun was shining and the wind was blowing. Ramal and Denzell took out their new bikes. Ramal's bike is loud red with platinum tires. Denzell has a regular Huffy blue bike. The girls were jumping rope and playing with their variety of baby dolls—some black, some white. The construction workers were finishing the house next door while cars passed by with red bows as if they got their car for Christmas.

FISK HOWARD ELEMENTARY SCHOOL

Rose is our neighborhood grocery store. It was named after the owner of the store's daughter, but the neighborhood calls all the family members Rose. It opens at 7:30 in the morning and closes twelve hours later. Rose are good people. They watch for you and your family, especially if you have little sisters and brothers. They'll let you go with a few cents if you are short. Sometimes if we need something, they'll let us go until my mom comes home.

Rose Grocery is so convenient for us. We don't have to go all over town to get a drink or something. We can just walk to the corner of Palmyra and Lopez where Rose is located. It has no restrictions on time. In other stores, you can't go in during school hours unless you have a parent or guardian with you over 18 years of age. Or, you can't come in until nine o'clock, which is after school starts. The Fisk Howard children stay in Rose's during the morning time trying to get their donuts and milk. As they leave they give the kids thanks and say, "I'll see you after school." Rachel and I interviewed Hien Pham right before the after-school rush.

AN INTERVIEW WITH HIEN PHAM

Rachel: What part of Vietnam is your family from?

Hien: South Vietnam.

R: What kind of work was your father doing there?

H: He worked for the CIA.

R: He worked for the CIA during the Vietnam War?

H: Yeah.

R: Why did your parents decided to move here?

H: I think the reason we moved because there was a war. We had to leave because of the change in government. If my dad would have stayed, he probably would have served time because he was in the military. Try to avoid prosecution.

R: Because he was working with the Americans he might have faced prosecution?

H: Yes.

R: Do you have any memories of Vietnam?

H: In the last eight years, I've been back there three times.

R: What keeps bringing you back?

H: Oh, we are visiting our relatives back there. And it's our home, you know. I try to go back there when we have a chance.

R: What are some things that are unique about Vietnam that you miss when you're in New Orleans?

H: I would say the atmosphere, the people. I think it's more around the same people. Like being at home.

R: What are some of the cultural differences between New Orleans and Vietnam?

H: Mmm. That's a good idea. The difference is we do things the old, traditional way. Clothes are hand-made instead of machine. The food especially—a lot of food that we have here that we don't have back there.

R: What are some of the things that Vietnamese immigrants in New Orleans might have had a hard time adjusting to since they've been here?

H: Well, at first, the language and trying to adjust to the culture. The climate is pretty much the same.

Actually, when we first came here we were in Pennsylvania. We stayed there with our sponsor for like a year or two, and then we had a friend of ours that lived here. They said that the weather was a lot better—it was almost the same as Vietnam—so we decide to move down here. Ever since we've been here.

R: Are y'all Catholic or are you Buddhist?

H: We're Catholic.

R: So how did y'all get involved with running Rose Grocery Store?

H: My dad he started off as a welder and then he had people who were doing fisherman, and they made more money doing it. He got into it for maybe ten years. He figured out that in the seafood business, it's not a yearly thing. My uncle, he had started [a grocery business] for two or three years, and that's how my dad got into it. He said you worked your own time, and it was more profitable. I would say it was a lot better than what he did before.

R: So how long have y'all had this store?

H: We've been in this store for about eighteen years.

R: So you guys came up with it?

H: When we started this business, we had to change

a lot of things in the store. It was a lot different. We were trying to get used to the neighborhood. At first it was difficult but through the years, we got along with everybody.

Q: What are some of the hard things about running a store and what are some of the good things?

H: Well, the hardest thing is that you have to have patience and try not to take everything personal. And try to work it out with your customer. Because when you deal with customers, you have different kinds of people and some are really hard on you, especially when they don't know you, they tend not to trust you. But once they know you, then they tend to trust you more and you get along with one another better.

R: The customers call everyone Rose?

H: Yeah, because it's easier instead of calling our name. The name Rose is actually the name of my youngest sister. And so the store is her name. Most of my customers know my real name.

R: Do they still call you Rose?

H: Yeah, I really don't care. I think it's easier to call Rose. It's easier to them: "Rose."

R: How long have you been working at the store?

H: Oh, I've been on and off, helping my dad, say fifteen years. On and off.

R: Do you see yourself staying in the grocery business?

H: Well, I like to but I think maybe by the end of this year we might give up the business and go on to something else.

R: What other things?

H: Actually, we have a couple of rental properties we have right now. And we'd like to probably do more of it. Probably get more into real estate, buying and selling, because it's more profitable. We'd probably invest [the store] in property.

R: What do you like to do on your free time?

H: On my free time I like to fix up my house. My wife and kids just bought a house and there's a lot of things that we need to change and fix it up and stuff.

R: Where do you live?

H: Oh, we live in Gretna.

R: How would describe the differences between Midcity and Gretna?

H: Midcity and Gretna? Gretna is more quiet than Midcity. It's peace and quiet down there.

Jana: This is the ghetto.

R: What do you like about having a store on Palmyra? What do you like about the neighborhood?

H: Well, I wouldn't say like, but the reason we work here is just to make money. I like everybody around here, you know. I mean, we get a long—occasionally we do have people who give trouble, but it's okay. We just don't take it personal. We're just the average people. You know, grocery, just trying to work hard, and we are straight honest people. You know. Just trying to make a living.

COOKING FOR LUCK IN THE NEW YEAR

We got up early to clean up. We had to make beds, dust furniture, and mop floors. We finished cleaning the house and went to the Carrollton shopping center. We went into Footlocker to purchase some shoes for my mother. We went to the Game Stop store to get some video games for my brother's X-Box game. My grandma called saying she wanted to go to Winn Dixie supermarket to purchase some cabbage and black-eyed peas. Afterwards we went to the Family Dollar Store to purchase some BC Goody powder for her headache and stopped by McDonald's to eat.

The next day our neighbors started getting ready to celebrate the New Year. All day they were cooking. They brought Bud Lights—the beer that they say tastes so good. They filled the ice cooler so much that the ice was falling over. My mama's and Ms. Nora's cabbage were competing. I couldn't decide which one smelled the best, but I know my mama's cabbage taste the best.

The neighbors were running back and forward to get my mama's cabbage. Once the neighborhood kids ate, they all went outside to pop fireworks. All you heard all night long was kick-krackle-pop, and of course gun shots. The police were over-protective in our neighborhood. They had police on each corner: Rendon, Lopez, and Jeff Davis. We were all thankful for that.

AN INTERVIEW WITH JOSE CRUZ

Jose is the handyman on Palmyra Street. Everyone calls on him to fix things. He also works at a jazz club in the French Quarter called the Palm Court Café. He's owned a big house on the block for 20 years. It's different because it's torn almost apart on the outside, but very neat on the inside. He didn't pay much for the house, but he cherishes it like diamonds and is trying to fix it up little by little. He has two daughters and two grandchildren. They all stay in the house along with a man named Paul. In this interview, we learn how he got to Palmyra Street from Puerto Rico.

A NUYORICAN IN MID-CITY

Jana: How long have you been livin here?

José: Twenty years.

J: Do you have any children?

Jo: I have two daughters, Jessica and Jennifer, and two grandsons named Jose and Pernell. Jennifer goes to LSU.

J: Where did you grow up?

Jo: In New York City, Brooklyn.

J: Did you like it out there?

Jo: Yeah, it was home for a while until I got old and decided to go to greener pastures.

J: That's where you are originally from?

Jo: Puerto Rico was where I was born. My mother brought us over to get a better education. She was a successful businesswoman in Puerto Rico. She had her own store and a restaurant, but I guess at that particular time and place, the educational system wasn't up to par. So let's go to Nueva York and see what they're doing! It's been like that ever since.

J: How old were you when you moved from Puerto Rico?

Jo: When I moved from Puerto Rico I was three years old. I spent the first twenty-five years of my life in New York.

J: What did your parents do?

Jo: My father was a butcher. He worked in the stockyards, which wasn't too far from our home. I used to recycle cardboard boxes to supplement my meager allowance as a child. And that paid two cents a pound. My mom worked as much as she could. She wasn't home when I came out of school. You know, most of the time we had to fend for ourselves.

J: What was your neighborhood like?

Jo: [I lived in] Williamsburg. Mainly it's a bunch of different people, talking a lot of different languages, but trying to get together. It was Italians, the Polish, the Jews, the blacks, and Hispanics. It's quite a melting pot of humanity. My friends [were] a little bit of everything: black, Spanish. white. The whole thing. It wasn't as complicated as now – things were a little more simple. I had fun. My best friend was a little black boy named Marshall. I used to take him home for lunch. We were tight like two peas in a pod.

I had to learn Spanish to speak to my parents, cuz they didn't speak no English. The young ones don't speak Spanish as well as they should. They're not exposed to it, and they don't have to learn it to communicate. But when it's a necessity, you'd be surprised how fast you learn. It's not a necessity now so everybody drags their feet.

J: Have you been back to Puerto Rico?

Jo: I've been back to Puerto Rico twice. Once for the '76 bicentennial. Being the patriot that I am, I've got to go back. And then I was there a couple of years ago. I hadn't seen my aunt in 25 years. She freaked out. I was her favorite nephew. I was only there a month. It's fun but there's not much work there.

It's a little island, you know. They live off tourism and stuff like that. They got a big Navy base from the U.S. that hires about three thousand people. Really, you could walk from one end of the island to the other in maybe a week. Hundred miles long and maybe fifty miles wide. It more or less fits in Lake Ponchartrain. You got three million people in that place. Half the people in Puerto Rico are from New

York. They fly back and forth, back and forth. Ninety percent of my relatives are in Puerto Rico. The other ten are in New York.

PALMYRA

Abram: And what made you come here?

Jo: My brother was a merchant seaman and he was shipping out of Jackson area. I was hitchhiking from California and I stopped over here and I've been here ever since.

A: How's it been for you?

Jo: It's been all right. I made a living. I've got a few good friends. Never had no serious problems with anybody. And other than that, I like the weather.

J: What do you miss about New York?

Jo: That's the culture capital on this side of the hemisphere. I miss the theatres and all that type of activity. I miss the Puerto Rican food: platanos, yucca–the stuff you get from the forest, off the land. Back then we ate basic things that kept us alive. You acquire a taste for it. [If] you cook it right, it don't taste too bad. I miss my mother's cooking more than anything.

J: What's it like living on Palmyra?

Jo: It's okay. I can't say it's hectic, but since I've been on the same block it's like a little community to me. And everybody looks out for me and I look out for them. So far, I've been lucky.

J: What do you like about the neighbors?

Jo: You know, they're friendly. It ain't like they don't care about you. If you present yourself in a certain manner, they'll respect you. And I respect my little neighborhood—Palmyra.

J: How did you buy this house?

Jo: The previous owner was robbed and tied up. You know, they ransacked the house, and they called the police to inform them that the lady's there. They came and untied her, and she went ahead and moved to Texas with her son.

I was living at 3212 Palmyra. My brother was selling the house and I was looking for a place. Being the inquisitive person that I am, I saw [this house] was empty and I checked the mail. It had a real estate listing. So I put it in my Dick Tracy bag, went over there, and asked [about it].

While she was alive, the owner let us stay here. She didn't worry about the rent. But when she died, her son says, "I want so much for rent," and since we didn't pay no rent, we saved that money [and] we had the down payment, and this is it. I was at the right place and God blessed me.

I got it for like twenty-five thousand. I could have gotten it with all the furniture, but I didn't know that. The guy was a very well off. He used to be the general manager of Maison Blanche back in the thirties and forties. He had old top of the line stuff, but I didn't know. I was just happy to get the house.

A: Was there a balcony on the second floor?

Jo: Yeah, but termites got it, so I took it off. We're

making plans to fix it. We'll bring it back to life. They got twenty-seven hundred square feet. Upstairs three bedrooms, two and half baths. We're comfortable here. I couldn't live like this in New York, that's for sure.

A: Yeah, really. It's a strange city where the dishwasher gets to own a mansion.

Jo: Well, this is more a humble home. We're fortunate. If you live right, you get your blessings down the road.

WORK

Jo: I work at the Palm Court Jazz Café at night.

J: What do you do there?

Jo: Oh, sanitation engineer.

A: You're in charge of keeping the place clean.

Jo: The dishwasher. They give you a fancy name; a fancy title.

J: Do you enjoy your job?

Jo: Oh, well, it's a job and if it were fun it would be called play. But it's a job, you know, you have to do it. Put your nose to the grindstone and just do it. I [also] do minor repairs. Odd and end jobs. Handyman.

GOOD DEEDS AND PUNISHMENTS

Rachel: One of the people that the other neighbors have been talking about is Paul. Can you describe Paul for us?

J: I'm lost for words. He's just a soul who threw away his life. Took everything for granted. Didn't plan ahead. He has no family and since I'm his only friend, Paul is the cross I have to bear.

His mother was from New Orleans and his father was from Honduras. He has a daughter and a son that he hasn't seen in twenty years—that I know of. And his life was just drinking, doing illicit drugs, and no proper hygiene. Just, literally, threw away his life. I don't know if he had a stroke or something. He has to be brain dead. Can't walk, can't talk. He can think a little bit. I have to cook for him and wash his clothes and stuff like that.

R: How did you meet?

We used to work together. He was a helper, noth-

ing technical. Can't read or write. And he stayed with my family for twelve years. He helped raise my daughters. And then he moved down to the Ninth Ward. You know, I said it's time for you to fly [from] the nest. I don't mind taking care of children. I don't mind taking care of people that need it. But he's a grown man. And it's time for him to grow up. But I guess he didn't, so he's in a second childhood.

R: He collects cans and things?

J: He collects cans. I tell him he has to go out, keep physical. You can't sit around and watch the big screen TV all day. You gotta keep moving, using your muscles and your brain to the best that you're capable of doing it. But, you know, to every good deed there's a punishment. That's what the Bible says. You know if I do something for somebody, just down the road I'm gonna get the shaft. That's how the ying and the yang work.

A: If you do something good you're going to get the shaft?

Jo: Yeah, it's just a matter of time. That's the level of life. If you do something, chances are somebody's going to do something bad to you. That's how it is. That's what makes people who care about people so special—they know it, but it doesn't stop them from caring. Cuz you might help somebody and he'll turn around and steal something for you. You know, that's how it is. It happens.

A: To me it seems like when I do a good turn by somebody, they often do a good turn back by me.

Jo: Yeah, but that's not the—

J: Norm.

Jo: Norm, yeah. That's an exception now and then. I say like, eight out of nine times, people take kindness for weakness. That's human nature.

A: Do you agree? People take kindness for weakness?

J: Yep. Yep.

Jo: "Oh, he's a nice guy; we'll put the shaft to him." Cuz, you know, if you're low down, they'll be scared of you, so they won't mess with you. That's what the Bible says. I'm glad that things are picking up.

A LITTLE KINDNESS HERE

A: How do you feel about the violence on Palmyra?

Jo: Well, it's changing now. In the twenty years I've been here, I know for a fact that nine people have been killed. The little boy who wrote to President Carter got shot down the block—I remember that. It was a sad state of affairs, but, it's like anything else, I could do my part and everybody has to do their part. But the people who do the crime don't live here. You know, the ones that make the neighborhood bad, they don't live here. They live somewhere else.

J: How do you feel about that?

Jo: Well, you can't really say anything. It's a free country. They have a right to go where they want, but I don't think it's right to do something to my neighborhood that they won't do in their neighborhood. Like sell drugs and everything else. They won't do that in front of their house but they'll come in front of your house and do it. It's a double standard or something.

J: How do you see the neighborhood changing in a few years?

Jo: Well, the property value went up. More families are comin in that have parents that work every day and contribute to society, as compared to the others one who don't contribute and just take, take. You know, but other than that, we're pretty lucky. No break-ins. No robberies or anything like that.

J: Okay. Can you tell us a story that happened on Palmyra?

Jo: I work a lot, but I got my neighbors to look out. Other than that, I never have witnessed a crime in action. But I take the little gestures of kindness that people do for me— the little things that matter in life. They look after my grandchildren if I'm busy. Oh, they make sure they don't cross the street. They keep an eye on my house. They say "Good morning. How you doin." Stuff like that. Nobody's going to do anything big, but a little kindness here, a little consideration there, and before you know it, you have a relationship with your families and your neighbors and the people in the city.

MR. RICKY AND EDDIE

During Mardi Gras, Eddie, Joseph, Ramal, and Lil Michael went to the Midcity Parade. Mr. Ricky and his sister Nora were sitting at the parade drinking their Budlight. Eddie didn't even know they were there until a float passed by throwing beads and cups. These big white pearls flew by, missed Eddie's hand, and hit Mr. Ricky in his face. Eddie quickly said, "I'm sorry" and they dapt it off with a hand shake. They stayed after the parade was over and Eddie, his friends, and Mr. Ricky went walking around. They bought all kinds of snacks like that sweet cotton candy. You know, the kind that melt in your hand, gets hard, and then you eat it? They bought super-long corn dogs and put ketchup and mustard all the way across it. After they ate, another parade was beginning to come down Canal Street toward Bourbon Street. You know, where all the wild people are. They had to be more careful and closer together.

The very next morning, Mr. Ricky knocked on the door for Eddie and asked him if he wanted to go fishing at Lake Pontchartrain. Eddie said yeah and got dressed. They went to the lake. It was a nice breezy day and the water was moving. The birds were flying over their heads. It was quiet. No unnecessary noise. All you heard was their small radio and CD player.

Ever since those outings, Eddie and Mr. Ricky have become close, close, close until they started doing outings all the time. Mr. Ricky started caring about Eddie as a nephew. That's why Eddie calls him "Uncle Ricky" and Ricky calls Eddie "Little Nephew."

Mr.Ricky

AN INTERVIEW WITH MARK DAMICO

Mark stays down the street from me. He has
two dogs and one cat. The cat gets along with the
dogs like best friends. He collects fireworks and
loves kites. I mean, all sorts of kites. He also builds
colorful flying rockets in his backyard. Most of the
time, though, he's working as a manager at Muriel's
in the French Quarter. He even does twenty-four
hour shifts non-stop. On his off days, he cleans up
and listens to music. It's the kind of music you play
at rave parties.

Mark is very nice. He offered me popcorn and a
Diet Coke before the interview. That's his favorite
snack. He enjoys life one day at a time and really
likes living on Palmyra Street.

FAMILY

Jana: Where are you from?

Mark: I was born in New Jersey, but I've lived all over the nation: Rhode Island, Ohio, Mississippi, Texas. My father was director of libraries at a lot of different universities. He was at Brown, the University of Dayton, Rice University. He was at the University of Southern Mississippi and then he retired at the University of South Alabama. I'm a library brat. My mother was the head of the history [or] English department wherever my father happened to be at.

J: How many brothers and sisters do you have?

M: I have two brothers: an older brother and a younger brother.

J: You're the middle one?

M: I'm the middle one. That's why I'm so weird. And we're all three so diverse—it's bizarre. My older brother is a raving right-wing Republican. And my little brother is like ultra-Christian longhaired Jesus Christ rocker. He's a recording engineer and he's in a heavy-metal Christian band called Lazarus.

WORK AND EDUCATION

M: It's really funny because education was so pushed on us. Everybody in my family has degrees except for

me. I went to college for eight years and was like, "You know what? This is not what I want to do. I don't want to go to college."

J: After eight years it went down the drain?

M: Oh, I didn't put it down the drain. I mean, I learned some stuff, but it's not what I want to be. I'm making more money now than some people with degrees make. But it's not about the money. It's about following what you want to do. Would I like to have a nine to five job sometimes? Yeah. You know, like around five o'clock when the sun is starting to get low and all the families are outside, I'm in absolute heaven. I'll take the dogs on the walk. It will just be beautiful out. But I never get to do that because I work so much. I work nights all the time.

J: Where do you work?

M: I'm the manager at Muriel's Jackson Square, which is a restaurant in the French Quarter. It's one of the oldest buildings in the city. The original structure went up in 1742. It's been sooo many things. It's been homes. It's been restaurants. It's been saloons. It's been a bordello. When they used to hold slave auctions in Jackson Square, they used to hold slaves in the carriage way. A lot of slaves would die there. It's one of the most haunted buildings in the city. We've seen hazy figures walking where floors used to be, we've seen little kid handprints, figures in the windows over looking Jackson Square.

J: Do you enjoy your job?

M: I enjoy my job sometimes. I hate the hours I work. Sometimes I work seventeen to twenty hours a day.

J: Why do you work so much?

M: Because in restaurants that's what you do. Restaurants are so busy that it requires constant management.

J: What do you do on your free time?

M: I'm a lover of electronic music. I collect fireworks ephemera and antique kites. My girlfriend and I are working on opening a bar here in town. I work too hard to be making so much money for somebody else, so we decided we were going to open a bar with a fireworks theme to it. It's going to be very cool. The bar is going to be called Rocket Lounge or Bang. I'm going to open it down in the Marigny.

DEEJAYING

J: What brought you to New Orleans?

M: Deejaying. I was in Hattiesburg, Mississippi and started deejaying college radio. I made a little bit of a name for myself, because I was in a small Southern town, and I was playing this really diverse stuff that caught the attention of a lot of record labels. This is 1982, 1983. It also caught the attention of a lot of acts. I really hated punk and I was always drawn to electronic music and deejaying and dancing. So I just kind of took it from there. When I graduated from high school, one of my friends was already a deejay down here and he taught me the ropes and I learned how to do it. Then the raves hit really big. Do you know what raves are? They're those big parties that they used to have at the State Palace. When raves became really big they just had a small pool of deejays to choose from and I just happened to be at the right place at the right time. I knew lots of friends who were doing music and they'd connect me with their friend and throwing this party here. I made the circuits. And then the next thing you know, "Oh, why don't you come over and do a gig over in London?" "Oh, we got this thing going on in Paris right now, why don't you come over tomorrow night and do it?" Literally, I'd fly in and fly out. I'd be in Paris for seven days.

Deejaying also leads into writing the music that deejays do and then I realized after doing it a number of years that my heart doesn't lie in trance and techno. It lies in down-tempo grooves—the head-bobbing chill-out stuff. The last time I ever played before an audience was at Love Parade. Love Parade is billed as the world's biggest party. It's in Berlin, Germany. You're not billed. It's just like whoever is there is there. They call you up and hire you. I played live before a million and half people. And to hear my music being played over an incredibly huge sound system and to see a million and a half people dancing to my music and screaming for it was an experience I had never done before and after I was done, I was like, You know what? I'll never ever be able to top this. So I retired from it completely.

SPIRITUALITY IN NEW ORLEANS

J: What is it like to live in New Orleans?

M: I've lived in New Orleans for twenty-five years. You know, I've been all over the world and something always brings me back. I think it's the fact that this city has a character unlike any other city on the face of this earth. Have you ever been to Vancouver? I lived there for two years and it was the cleanest city; everybody's healthy, everybody's good-looking. There's no crime. The cops had to shoot a guy who was attacking with scissors one day and it was headline news for a week because there's zero crime. It was environmentally friendly, which I'm really very much into the environment, but the city has absolutely zero soul. There's a filthiness to this city that keeps you here. It's depth. It has atmosphere you can touch. It's pristine in it's dirtiness. It's like we celebrate the fact that this city is—

J: Dirty.

M: I don't mean dirty in this like, "Ick, it's dirty." It's just like, it's grimey and it's gritty and it smells like swamps and gunpowder, and tar and red beans. It's just a mixture of everything good and bad you can imagine. And it completely evens it out. The city has a soul. It has a very spiritual sense to it. I don't mean spiritual in the religious sense.

J: What's your religion?

M: Agnostic. Do you know what agnostic is? I do

believe in God and I don't follow any certain religion. You know, I was raised Catholic and Catholicism will always be a part of my culture. Like I feel very comfortable in the Catholic Church. I feel comfortable around other Catholics. There's a lot of ceremony involved with it and I feel comfortable with that because that's how I was raised, but I don't necessarily believe the teachings of the Church. I don't believe what the church states that we should believe. But I do believe in God. I'm very spiritual. I do pray. I just try to be a good person.

PALMYRA STREET

J: How long have you been living here?

M: One year.

J: What it's like to live on Palmyra Street?

M: I've lived all over the city of New Orleans and so far this has been my favorite place. Before I was living here I was living uptown on Panola Street. I was paying about twelve hundred bucks a month. I had fifteen-foot ceilings, two stories—it was beautiful. And I was like, "You know what? I want a little bit more culture." I found this place, and immediately the first day I moved in, [a neighbor's] asking for five dollars for cigarettes and a beer. And I was like, "This is where I want to be. This is very cool."

When I first moved into this neighborhood, people were like, "Oh, you're moving to the hood. You're moving into the worst neighborhood in the city." I'm like, "No I'm not. I'm moving into a great neighborhood." I love the feel of Midcity. You know, I like being close to the park. I like being close to Bayou St. John so the doggies can swim.

J: What do you like about the neighbors?

M: I like the fact that the neighborhood is culturally diverse. It's a mishmash of every culture. You've got Asian, you got Latin, you got African-American, you got me, you got everybody.

J: You?

M: And how do you classify me for God's sake! The other day I was outside talking to Kristy, my girlfriend, and the kids [across the street] were on the porch saying, "This is a black neighborhood, you should leave. This is a black neighborhood, you need to leave."

J: Ohhh!

M: I know. "Do I look black? I'm here." I didn't get them. They didn't like me. I bought them M&Ms; now they like me. I like the fact that it's many, many families that live in this neighborhood. I'm on a first name basis with a lot of the children. Most of the neighbors know me by name, even though I'm rarely at home because I work so much. I love the fact that when I first moved here all the neighbors thought I was a cop—which still perplexes me.

J: I did, too.

M: You thought I was a cop, too. Every person did. There's so many different characters in this neighborhood. I know my neighborhood crack dealer. He brings in my garbage cans in for God's sake. And crazy Paul across street. The other day I walked out, he had a crowbar and he's like shoving it down the sewer. I'm like, "Mr. Paul what are you doin?" He's like, "AHEHEH." He was looking for a cigarette he'd dropped down the sewer. So I gave him a cigarette.

I came home from work and he was sitting on that pick-up truck. He had this huge gash on his face and all this blood was flowing. I was like, "God, Mr. Paul what the hell happened?" Someone hit him in the face with a brick and completely split his face. So I'm like, you know, who else is going to take care of it? He doesn't remember what he's saying half the time. So I go inside, I soak this rag full of alcohol. I take this alcohol filled rag and put it over his face and I put a cigarette in his mouth and then I light it. And then I realize, "You know what? I'm just putting this flame by this alcohol soaked rag. This guy is going to go up flames." He doesn't care. Anyway, he's just sitting here with this rag and cigarrete hanging out of his mouth. He's like, "I call her a black bitch." I gave him a Corona which really kind of calmed him down. From the outside it doesn't look like the best neighborhood. I mean, look at Jose's house.

J: It looks good on the inside.

M: Oh, it's beautiful on the inside. That's one of the main reasons I live over on this street. And that's how I would describe this street. You know who used to own that house?

J: Who?

M: The guy who was the general manager of Maison Blanche in the fifties.

SAFETY

J: What do you think about the crime around Palmyra?

M: I didn't know there was any.

J: You didn't?

M: I'm at work all the time. I will say this. Who lives here on the corner? Across the street where the kids are on the porch all the time upstairs? Since I've moved here a year, I've counted the fire trucks there six or seven times. I'm not sure if someone's sick over there, but there's fire trucks
there all time.

J: No, it's not upstairs, it's downstairs. Ms. Ruth—she's sick.

M: Oh, she's sick. Is there a lot crime on this street? Holy crap, I didn't know that! Like what's going on?

J: Like, there's been killings and everything.

ANIMALS

J: Do you have any children?

M: I have no children. I have two dogs, which I love very dearly—Betty Pasgetti and Ooby Dooby Do. Like these little kids say, "Pasgetti." Do you want to meet her?

J: No.

M: She's so friendly.

J: I don't like dogs.

M: I promise, I promise—come here Betty! Are you scared of dogs?

J: Yeah!

M: Just trust me. Here's my good girl Betty. See,

she's trying to figure out who you are. That's the neighbor. She doesn't like the little girls. Are those your nieces or cousins or something? The three little girls?

J: No, that's the next-door neighbors.

M: They terrorize her. They'll come to the gate, yell at her, and run away when she starts barking. I also adopted one of your cats. I opened the door one day, and Mickey Blue Eyes was standing there. "Meow. Meow." Not even that loud; a little kitten yell.

"Oh, my God. Who are you? Where were you? Come to visit?" As soon as I opened the door, he came right inside and went to the dogs' water bowl and started drinking. So he's been with us since. He's been raised by the dogs so he acts like a dog. "Come on guys!" All three of em come runnin.

J: We only have two left.

M: The people from Manuel's Tamales catch them and put them in their tamales.

J: No.

M: It's the truth. I heard it from a sixth grader!

J: They steal em.

M: Well, one of em showed up on my door, but I don't know if that's stealing. He came to me. He's a good kitty. But he follows me, which is really starting to get annoying. I walked the dogs to Walgreeen's the other day and there was Micky. He had crossed Canal Street. I mean, how dangerous is that? He's going to get smashed. I'll be in the neutral ground and here comes kitty just bounding down Jeff Davis. He doesn't know his own boundaries. Stupid cat. He thinks he's a dog.

CHANGES

J: How do you see the neighborhood changing in the next few years?

M: Yeah, it's going to be very upper-middle class. That's because the streetcar's moved in apparently. I think a lot of white families are going to move in. I think a lot of the African-American and Latino families that own these homes are going to be offered unGodly sums of the money for their homes and won't be able to turn it down. Mr. Paul on the corner could get over $200,000 dollars for his house. They sold this one for $150,000. My rent will probably shoot up to $700, $800, $900 a month in the next few years. I think that was the change.

Some people would say it's changing it for the better, but I don't necessarily see that for the better. I don't see that as a better thing for the neighborhood. Look at all the families here. Look at the kids playing next door. I mean, yeah, that drives me up the wall sometimes when they really start screaming. Where are the cool people supposed to go? The Marigny's up and coming, Treme's up and coming. All these old cool neighborhoods are becoming upper white middle class. There's no place for us to go anymore.

J: Who's going to live in [the other side of your house?] You don't know? What's the rent going to be on it?

M: Probably eight hundred.

M: I don't know how a family lives in a shotgun. I lived in this house with one person and I was going up the wall, because you have no place to go. If she had people over, it's like, I'd have to close the bedroom door, but I could still hear them cutting up in the living room. It was miserable. This is the perfect house for one person.

J: I always did have to share a room with my sister. I don't know what it is to have a room to myself.

M: You will one day, dear. And you will be the happiest girl that's ever lived.

J: They want all of us to go to the projects.

M: I would go to the projects if they let me bring my dogs and I can still recycle.

J: I've never lived in the projects.

M: When I used to ride my bike down Freret [past] the Magnolia Projects] and all of a sudden I felt a really sharp pain on the side of my head. Someone had thrown a broken bottle at me. All I was doin was ridin my bike.

J: Do you still ride your bike?

M: Oh, man, I was run over by a bus while I was riding my bike. Right on Canal Street. I was crossing Canal Street at Camp and a bus just plowed right over me. "I didn't even see you, man. I didn't even see you." You know what's funny about that? The most distinct memory of being run over on my bike was the sound the bus made when it ran over the bell. I was underneath the bus and I was kicking myself away from the tires so it wouldn't run over me, and when the tires ran over the bell it was like, "Ching!" Isn't that weird? Oh, I've had quite an interesting life. Okay, shall we continue? I digress.

RESISTANCE

When I was in Hattiesburg, Mississippi, I lived in the most bizarre place. The southern white Baptists there are just like this fraternity of idiots. They bought this entire neighborhood [and] tore down all the houses and built parking lots and church buildings. The lady that owned my house refused to sell it. Mrs. Willie Mae Bird. "I ain't going to sell to that" church. And I swear on my death bed."

She died in the house and made her daughter swear she would never sell it. So here I was—this little tiny house, surrounded by this huge church complex. Apparently, she loved the house so much she didn't want to leave it. The first night in the house, my three cats were all sitting on the edge of the bed growling down the hallway [with their fur] all puffed up. I had the covers up around my chin. Ms. Willie Mae was looking at me down the hallway. She was making her presence known.

THE NEIGHBORHOOD STORY PROJECT
OUR STORIES TOLD BY US

What you have just read is one of the five books to come from the first year of the Neighborhood Story Project. This has been an incredible year for us, and we thank you for your support and attention.

The Neighborhood Story Project would like to give a big shout out to the people of the City of New Orleans—y'all are the best. Thank you for showing so much love.

There are lots of folks and organizations that have made this possible. You have come through with stories, with food, with love, and with money—and believe us when we say that all four are necessary.

First off, we'd like to acknowledge our great partners, the Literacy Alliance of Greater New Orleans and the University of New Orleans. Specifically, Peg Reese, Rachel Nicolosi, Rick Barton, Tim Joder, Bob Cashner, Susan Krantz and Jeffrey Ehrenreich have been excellent supervisors and colleagues.

To Steve Gleason and Josselyn Miller at the One Sweet World Foundation. Thank-you for getting this project from the very beginning, and for having such awesome follow through.

To the institutions of the city that have been good to us—thank you. Good institutions play such an important role in making a place. Specifically we'd like to thank the Greater New Orleans Foundation, The Lupin Foundation, The Louisiana Endowment for the Humanities, Tulane Service Learning, The Schweser Family Foundation, and the guys from the Cultivating Community Program for donating the proceeds from your work with Longue Vue to help us get these books out.

To all of the individuals who have stepped up and given so much—from the donation of stamps to all the folks who have trusted us with their money. To Phyllis Sassoon and Mick Abraham for donating their cars. To all the folks who contributed, from the change jars at Whole Foods to the checks and food donations.

Thanks to our incredible steering committee, GK Darby, Peter Cook, Norbert Estrella, Tim Lupin, and Eliza Wells.

To Kalamu ya Salaam and Jim Randels at SAC, for taking us in and showing us the ropes, and giving us support as we try to grow. If we have done anything right as teachers it is because you have taught us.

To the administration of John McDonogh Senior High, Principal Spencer, and the past principals Winfield and Goodwin, thank you for being such great partners. To Ms. Pratcher and Ms. Tuckerson, thank you and bless you for dealing with all the headaches we cause. And to the staff at John McDonogh, we are so proud to be working with you.

To Elena Reeves and Kenneth Robin at the Tchopshop, thanks for being great designers, and for being such great sports about working with us. And to Jenny LeBlanc and Kyle Bravo at Hot Iron Press, thank you for being great designers/printer and for moving to town.

To Lauren Schug and Heather Booth, for transcribing and transcribing, above and beyond the call of duty.

To Anita Yesho for copy editing at short notice.

To Stephanie Oberhoff, and Communities in Schools- your mission is beautiful and your execution is great.

To Beverly McKenna, thank you for giving us such a beautiful office when we were only a sliver of an idea.

To Gareth Breunlin, who laid out the books and designed the covers. You have made our ideas come out on paper in a way that has honored all of the work and love involved.

To Davey and Jamie for being our dogs.

To Jerry for grant-writing, copy-editing, and being our hero.

To Dan, for his constant input, sharing a car and a computer, writing grants and cooking numerous dinners for the NSP.

To Shana, for promoting this project like it was your own, and for the input and help and grace.

And our biggest thank-you and respect to all of the Bolding, Jackson, Nelson, Price, and Wylie families. Without your love and care, this would not have been possible. Thank you for believing in the project and the work, and for making these books what they are.

And to Palmyra, Lafitte, St. Claude, Dorgenois (and the rest of Ebony's Sixth Ward), and N. Miro, thank you for your stories. We hope you like the books as much we liked making them.

The list is so long because so many of you have contributed.

Thanks for reading.

For the Neighborhood Story Project

Rachel Breunlin
Abram Himelstein

P.S. Thanks to Richard Nash, Ammi Emergency and Soft Skull Press for believing in us and New Orleans in our time of need.